1st Workshop on Automatic Text Adaptation (ATA 2018)

Tilburg, The Netherlands
8 November 2018

ISBN: 978-1-5108-7754-2

Printed from e-media with permission by:

Curran Associates, Inc.
57 Morehouse Lane
Red Hook, NY 12571

Some format issues inherent in the e-media version may also appear in this print version.

Printed by Curran Associates, Inc. (2019)

Association for Computational Linguistics
209 N. Eighth Street
Stroudsburg, Pennsylvania 18360

Phone: 1-570-476-8006
Fax: 1-570-476-0860

acl@aclweb.org

Additional copies of this publication are available from:

Curran Associates, Inc.
57 Morehouse Lane
Red Hook, NY 12571 USA
Phone: 845-758-0400
Fax: 845-758-2633
Email: curran@proceedings.com
Web: www.proceedings.com

ATA 2018

The 1st Workshop on Automatic Text Adaptation

Proceedings of the Workshop

November 8, 2018
Tilburg, The Netherlands

Order copies of this and other ACL proceedings from:

Association for Computational Linguistics (ACL)
209 N. Eighth Street
Stroudsburg, PA 18360
USA
Tel: +1-570-476-8006
Fax: +1-570-476-0860
acl@aclweb.org

Introduction

This volume contains the papers presented at W18-70 1st Workshop on Automatic Text Adaptation (ATA) held on November 8, 2018 in conjunction with INLG 2018 in Tilburg.

The aim of the workshop was to bring together researchers interested in techniques for adapting texts to the needs for various users and NLP applications. This includes studies of end users' needs for text adaptation, techniques for automatic text adaptation, user evaluation of adapted texts, and infrastructure for conducting research on text adaptation.

We invited the text adaptation community and researchers and practitioners working on generating texts tailored to populations with specific needs. Examples of these include text simplification, as well as adaptation to the needs of second-language learners, and relevant applications from other areas such as machine translation, information extraction, virtual assistants, and accessibility research.

Arne Jönsson, Evelina Rennes, Horacio Saggion, Sanja Štajner, Victoria Yaneva
November 2018

Workshop Organizers:

Arne Jönsson, Linköping University
Evelina Rennes, Linköping University
Horacio Saggion, Universitat Pompeu Fabra
Sanja Štajner, University of Mannheim
Victoria Yaneva, University of Wolverhampton

Program Committee:

Thomas François, Université Catholique de Louvain
Núria Gala, Aix-Marseille Université
David Kauchak, Pomona College
Ildiko Pilan, Gothenburg University
Maja Popovic, ADAPT Centre @ DCU
Carolina Scarton, University of Sheffield
Ineke Schuurman, Katholieke Universiteit Leuven
Leen Sevens, Katholieke Universiteit Leuven
Irina Temnikova, Qatar Computing Research Institute
Sowmya Vajjala, Iowa State University
Elena Volodina, Gothenburg University
Ingrid Zukerman, Monash University

Invited Speaker:

Thomas François, Université Catholique de Louvain

Table of Contents

Workshop Program

Thursday, November 8, 2018

8:30–9:00	Registration
9:00–9:10	Welcome
9:10–10:10	Invited Talk
10:10–10:30	*Study of Readability of Health Documents with Eye-tracking Approaches* Natalia Grabar, Emmanuel Farce and Laurent Sparrow
10:30–11:00	Coffee Break
11:00–11:20	*Reference-less Quality Estimation of Text Simplification Systems* Louis Martin, Samuel Humeau, Pierre-Emmanuel Mazaré, Éric De La Clergerie, Antoine Bordes and Benoît Sagot
11:20–11:40	*Assisted Lexical Simplification for French Native Children with Reading Difficulties* Firas Hmida, Mokhtar B. Billami, Thomas François and Núria Gala
11:40–12:00	*CLEAR – Simple Corpus for Medical French* Natalia Grabar and Rémi Cardon
12:00–12:20	*Improving Machine Translation of English Relative Clauses with Automatic Text Simplification* Sanja Štajner and Maja Popovíc

Invited talk

The Interface between Readability and Automatic Text Simplification: Identifying Difficulties to Support Simple Writing

Thomas François

Assistant Professor at CENTAL, IL&C (UCLouvain)

For nearly a century, readability formulas have focused on the complex task of outputing a single numerical value consisting in an estimate of the difficulty of a text for a given population of readers. Although this synthetic approach has virtues in certain contexts, its main limitation is that it analyses how dozens or even hundreds of linguistic characteristics of a text affect the reading process, but lets the user know about this process only through this single numerical value. Automatic text simplification (ATS), for its part, aims to identify complex features in a text (words, syntactic structures, numbers, etc.) and automatically simplify them. Despite being a finer-grained approach, due to the lack of theoretical and empirical data, ATS still struggles to identify all linguistic characteristics that should be simplified.

In this talk, we will first set out our view of both fields and their current limitations in more details. In a second step, we will present several projects that are located at the interface between text readability and ATS, including the CEFRLex project (`http://cental.uclouvain.be/cefrlex/`), which is a set of lexical resources that can be used for readability and ATS purposes, the AMesure project (`http://cental.uclouvain.be/amesure/`), a platform to support simple writing of administrative texts, and ReSyf (`https://cental.uclouvain.be/resyf/`), which is a disambiguated and graded resource with synonyms. These projects will illustrate how automatically detecting complex segments of texts using readability techniques can inform semi-supervised or unsupervised simplification systems.

Bio: Thomas François is an Assistant Professor at UCLouvain (`http://cental.fltr.ucl.ac.be/team/tfrancois/`) in Applied Linguistics. His research focuses on readability, text simplification, automatic complex word identification, and efficient communication in professional contexts. He completed his Ph.D. at the Centre for Natural Language Processing (CENTAL, UCLouvain) and has received the best Ph.D. Thesis award by the ATALA in 2012. He spent a one-year research stay at IRCS (University of Pennsylvania) as a B.A.E.F. and Fulbright Fellow. As a follow up, he returned to UCLouvain and benefited from several post-doctoral research scholarships at CENTAL (founded by the FNRS and several regional projects such as iMediate and SPORTIC), before becoming a member of the UCLouvain academic staff. He has led projects such as CEFRLex (`http://cental.uclouvain.be/cefrlex/`), a CEFR-graded lexicon for foreign language learning or AMesure (`http://cental.uclouvain.be/amesure/`), a platform to support simple writing. He has also organized the CL4LC workshop, and has been invited to review for several NLP conferences (ACL, Coling, NAACL), journals (Computational Linguistics, ELRA), or book series (Synthesis Lectures on Human Technologies).

Proceedings of the 1st Workshop on Automatic Text Adaptation (ATA), pages 1–2,
Tilburg, The Netherlands, November 8 2018.

CLEAR – Simple Corpus for Medical French

Natalia Grabar, Rémi Cardon
CNRS, UMR 8163, F-59000 Lille, France;
Univ. Lille, UMR 8163 - STL - Savoirs Textes Langage, F-59000 Lille, France
natalia.grabar@univ-lille.fr, remi.cardon@univ-lille.fr

Abstract

Availability of corpora with technical and simplified contents is crucial for the development and test of methods for text simplification. We describe this kind of corpus for the French medical language. The corpus contains texts from three sources: encyclopedia, drug leaflets and scientific summaries. Each source proposes comparable information in specialized and plain languages. A subset of this corpus has been processed manually in order to find and align parallel sentences. This subset currently contains 663 pairs with parallel sentences. Alignment has been done by two annotators and shows 0.76 inter-annotator agreement. The corpus with comparable data is available for research (http://natalia.grabar.free.fr/resources.php).

1 Introduction

Research performed in text simplification provides tools and resources for the creation of simplified versions of texts. Simplification can be positioned at different levels (*ie.* lexical, syntactic, semantic, pragmatic and structural). It can be useful for different kinds of human users: children (Son et al., 2008; De Belder and Moens, 2010; Vu et al., 2014), foreigners or poor-readers (Paetzold and Specia, 2016), people with neurodegenerative disorders (Chen et al., 2016), lay people reading specialized documents (Arya et al., 2011; Leroy et al., 2013). In these cases, simplification may guarantee a better access to the contents of documents. Simplification may also be exploited as a pre-processing step of documents undergoing other NLP treatments: syntactic analysis (Chandrasekar and Srinivas, 1997; Jonnalagadda et al., 2009), semantic annotation (Vickrey and Koller, 2008), summarization (Blake et al., 2007), machine translation (Stymne et al., 2013; Štajner and Popović, 2016), indexing (Wei et al., 2014), information retrieval and extraction (Beigman Klebanov et al., 2004). The purpose is then to provide more easily processable versions of text and to improve the overall results of NLP tools.

Often, the feasibility and success of such works depend on the existence of the required corpora. Yet, in some languages and specialized fields such corpora may be missing.

The purpose of our work is to introduce and describe the CLEAR corpus, which gathers complex and simplified versions of documents related to medical topics in French. In what follows, we first present some existing work in corpora building for simplification (Section 2), we then describe our contribution to this area (Sections 3 and 4), and conclude (Section 5).

2 Corpora for Simplification

If the first works in development of simplification tools have mainly relied on manually crafted simplification rules following the linguistic intuition of researchers (Chandrasekar et al., 1996; Siddharthan, 2006; Max, 2008), recent works are mostly guided by linguistic data and rely on dedicated corpora. Most often, parallel corpora are exploited in this task. They provide original texts together with their simplified versions. Sometimes, aligned corpora are also available, in which the correspondence is done at the level of sentences. This kind of corpora provide direct correspondence between complex and simple (or simplified) sentences. Notice that comparable corpora, containing complex and simple documents addressing the same topics, are more easily available but require specific methods or pre-processings before

Proceedings of the 1st Workshop on Automatic Text Adaptation (ATA), pages 3–9,
Tilburg, The Netherlands, November 8 2018. ©2018 Association for Computational Linguistics

they can be exploited for simplification work.

Several parallel corpora for several languages have been created, mainly thanks to the manual simplification of their contents: Spanish (Bott et al., 2014), Italian (Brunato et al., 2014), Brazilian Portuguese (Caseli et al., 2009), Danish (Klerke and Sgaard, 2012), and of course English (Chandrasekar and Srinivas, 1997; Daelemans et al., 2004; Petersen and Ostendorf, 2007; Specia et al., 2012). Yet, these parallel corpora are seldom freely available. Some of these corpora also explicitly indicate what has been simplified and how (removal, segmentation...). Hence, a multi-axial annotation schema has been proposed for this purpose with several simplification classes: split, merge, reorder, insert (verbs, subjects and other components), delete (verbs, subjects and other components), transform (lexical substitution, replacement of anaphora, noun-verb, verb-noun, passive-active, verbal features...) (Brunato et al., 2014). This annotation schema covers lexical and syntactic simplification.

Comparable corpora of this kind are also available, among which the most frequently used is the pair built with English Wikipedia[1] and English Simple Wikipedia[2]. This corpus is widely used by researchers (Zhu et al., 2010; Biran et al., 2011; Coster and Kauchak, 2011). A similar comparable corpus also exists in French and can be built fromq French Wikipedia[3] and Vikidia[4], which has been created for children. This source in French has been used for the detection of rules for syntactic transformations (Brouwers et al., 2012). Besides, researchers working on English also exploit history of revisions of articles from Simple Wikipedia (Yatskar et al., 2010), simplified versions of scientific articles[5] (Elhadad and Sutaria, 2007), simplified versions of novels [6] (Vajjala and Meurers, 2015), as well as simplified versions of educational and news articles[7].

[1]https://en.wikipedia.org/wiki/Main_Page

[2]https://simple.wikipedia.org/wiki/Main_Page

[3]https://fr.wikipedia.org

[4]https://fr.vikidia.org

[5]http://www.reutershealth.com

[6]www.onestopenglish.com

[7]https://newsela.com/

3 Comparable Medical Simplified French Corpus

For the building of the corpus, we propose to exploit three types of French sources related to the medical field: articles from online encyclopedia (Section 3.1), drug leaflets with drug description and their optimal use (Section 3.2), and summaries from systematic reviews as provided by the Cochrane collaboration (Section 3.3). These sources provide documents from different textual genres: encyclopedia articles, scientific articles and drug description close to clinical texts. These three sources are available under free license (license not allowing modifications of the data in the case of the Cochrane reviews), and can be used for research purposes. Finally, these sources provide comparable corpora, distinguished by their technicality, on different topics: medical topics in encyclopedia, various drugs in drug leaflets, and questions related to treatment and diagnosis of disorders in Cochrane summaries. A part of these data have been aligned manually at the level of sentences (Section 4).

3.1 Encyclopedia Articles

This source provides articles from two collaborative encyclopedia in French available online: Wikipedia and Vikidia. French Wikipedia is intended for French-speaking people, while Vikidia has been created for providing similar information for 8 to 13 year old children. These two encyclopedia provide articles on a great variety of topics: politics, economics, medecine, culture, geography, etc. Wikipedia shows a better coverage than Vikidia: it is older and more popular. Creation of articles in these encyclopedia has to respect precise guidelines: they must be clear and understandable, be formal, with no use of jargon from specialized areas. Yet, as Vikidia is intended for children, the articles must contain as well: simple definitions and introduction, clear development, examples, sources and external links, and, if possible, pictures, schema, audio and video. It is also suitable to make children participate in the creation of the articles[8]. Even if articles from these two sources may be related to common topics, they are created independently from each other.

Articles from encyclopedia have been collected from the corresponding dumps in September 2017

[8]https://fr.vikidia.org/wiki/Aide:Comment_cr%C3%A9er_un_article

for Wikipedia and in August 2017 for Vikidia. Overall, Wikipedia contains 1,906,251 articles, and Vikidia contains 46,721 articles. Among the Wikipedia articles, we keep only 20,972 articles related to medicine and the medical portal. Among these, 575 articles exist in Wikipedia and Vikidia with identical titles. These 575 topics and pairs of articles are collected for building the corpus. Wikipedia articles contain 2,293,078 word occurrences, and Vikidia articles contain 197,672 word occurrences.

3.2 Drug Leaflets

Each drug marketed in France is provided together with a leaflet describing for instance its composition, prescription indications, known adverse effects, and precautions. This information is created in two versions. One version is intended for health professionals, and contains technical and comprehensive information on a given drug. Besides, this version presents a specific structure and makes use of a very rich medical terminology. Another version is intended for patients, and contains essential and simplified information on drugs. The style is personal. It addresses the patient directly and commonly using expressions like *votre santé* (your health), *votre médecin* (your physician), or *vous pouvez* (you can). Information is structured as questions and answers: *Qu'est-ce que c'est ?* (What is this?), *Quels sont les effets indésirables éventuels ?* (What are the possible adverse effects?). These simplified versions are created systematically for each marketed drug, and later inserted into the drug boxes.

This corpus is built from documents available in the *public drug base*[9] managed by the Ministry of Health in France. These documents have been downloaded in June 2017. The corpus contains 11,800 drugs with technical and simplified leaflets. The technical part contains 52,313,126 word occurrences, and the simplified part contains 33,682,889 word occurrences.

3.3 Cochrane Summaries

The purpose of the Cochrane foundation is to provide high evidence medical information (Sackett et al., 1996). For several years, researchers of the domain have been working on creation of systematic reviews on various medical questions often in relation with diagnostics and treatment of disorders. Existing work on a given question are collected and read by experts. A synthesis is created, which methodological and scientific validity is higher than the one of each individual work. This also provides information with a higher evidence for medical professionals. For each extensive review, a short summary is also created. In addition to technical summaries for the experts, simplified summaries (*Plain language summary*) are created for lay people.

This corpus is built with documents available on the online library of Cochrane[10]. The documents have been downloaded in November 2017. The corpus contains 8,789 systematic reviews. Among these, 3,815 reviews provide technical and simplified versions of summaries. The technical part of the corpus contains 2,840,003 word occurrences and the simplified part contains 1,515,051 word occurrences.

4 Parallel Medical Simplified French Corpus

A subset of the whole comparable corpus has been aligned at the level of sentences. We randomly selected 14 encyclopedia articles, 12 drug leaflets, and 13 Cochrane summaries. The alignment has been performed manually by two annotators with the NLP training and used to the medical area texts. We have determined several criteria for alignment or non-alignment of two sentences, technical and simplified. They are illustrated with examples from the *Cochrane* corpus:

1. Identical sentences and sentences varying only by punctuation or stopwords are not aligned. Even if such pairs of sentences provide very close or identical semantic contents, we consider indeed that such pairs are not helpful for the creation of transformation rules useful for the simplification of contents;

2. Sentences within an aligned pair must have the same or very close meaning (semantic equivalence), and they must show lexical and/or syntactic adaptations, at least:
   - *Preterm infants are at risk of periventricular haemorrhage (PVH).*
   - *Babies born very early (before 34 weeks) are at risk of bleeding in the brain (periventricular haemorrhage).*

[9] `http://base-donnees-publique.medicaments.gouv.fr/`

[10] `http://www.cochranelibrary.com/`

		Technical				*Simplified*			
		source		*aligned*		*source*		*aligned*	
corpus	*doc.*	*sent.*	*occ.*	*sent.*	*occ.*	*sent.*	*occ.*	*sent.*	*occ.*
Drug	12*2	4,416	44,709	502	5,751	2,736	27,820	502	10,398
Cochrane	13*2	553	8,854	112	3,166	263	4,688	112	3,306
Encyclopedia	14*2	2,494	36,002	49	1,100	238	2,659	49	853

Table 1: Size of the reference data and their consensual alignment at the level of sentences.

3. The meaning of one sentence can be fully included in another sentence. This is the case of semantic inclusion. In the following example, the content of the simplified sentence is included in the technical sentence:

    - *We found no studies that reported the effect of whole grain diets on total cardiovascular mortality or cardiovascular events (total myocardial infarction, unstable angina, coronary artery bypass graft surgery, percutaneous transluminal coronary angioplasty, total stroke).*
    - *We found no studies reporting on the effect of whole grains on deaths from cardiovascular disease or cardiovascular events.*

4. Semantic intersection, where each sentence of the pair brings its own additional information, is not accepted:

    - *However, over the past two decades endovascular aneurysm repair (EVAR) has gained popularity as a treatment option.*
    - *However, over the past 20 years, a newer, 'key hole' technique has been used, in which the AAA is repaired without the need for open surgery - a thin tube is passed via the blood vessels in the groin to the site of the AAA.*

The alignment has been done independently by two annotators. Agreement occurs when the annotators propose the same alignment of sentences, and disagreement occurs when a given pair is only aligned by one of the annotators. As a second step, the disagreements are discussed in order to reach the consensus when possible. As a result, a given pair of sentences can be approved for the alignment or rejected.

Table 1 indicates the size of the source and aligned sets with consensual alignments. We obtain a total of 663 pairs of aligned sentences. This is a small set of parallel data, but it is intended to grow up thanks to the design and use of suitable models for the automatic alignment of sentences. The 663 already aligned pairs of sentences provide the necessary reference data.

Semantic annotation is one of the hardest annotation tasks and usually shows low annotation agreement (Artstein and Poesio, 2008), which has been particularly highlighted for word sense tagging (Véronis, 1998; Mihalcea et al., 2004; Palmer et al., 2007). Hence, the annotation of semantic closeness between two sentences is also complicated. In our experiment, the inter-rater agreement is 0.76 (Cohen, 1960). It is computed within the set of the aligned sentences from the two annotators. Such inter-annotator agreement is qualified as substantial according to the usual interpretation scale (Landis and Koch, 1977) and may indicate a good reliability of the obtained data.

Another interesting point is related to the parallelism between the technical and simple versions of documents. It has been indeed observed that the degree of parallelism in comparable corpora may vary from almost parallel corpora, with many parallel sentences, to very-non-parallel corpora (Fung and Cheung, 2004). In the CLEAR corpus, we can observe that aligned sentences are rarer in the *Drugs* and *Encylopedia* corpora than in the *Cochrane* corpus. Indeed, these three sources have different principles involved during the creation of their contents:

- Summaries of systematic reviews from Cochrane are intentionally simplified by researchers starting from the original technical summaries;
- Vikidia articles are written independently from Wikidia articles, even if they address the same topics: there is no adaptation of one content into another. Besides, as Vikidia articles are created for children, their content is adapted for them;

- In the *Drugs* corpus, the same drugs are described for health professionals and for patients, which provides good common ground. Yet, several kinds of information are specific either to the professional version (precise composition, action on the organism, molecules, detailed information on adverse effects...) or to the patient's (precautions of use, warnings...).

It would be interesting to formalize the notion of parallelism between two corpora, which should be indicative of the rate of parallel sentences they may provide.

The first observations of parallel sentences indicate that they provide mainly syntactic and lexical transformations, and that the simplification principles differ according to the document sources. For instance, sentence splitting is applied in drug leaflets and encyclopedia articles, while the sentences are usually merged during the simplification process in Cochrane summaries. These and other simplification features are being analyzed. They will allow to propose adaptation rules that apply at lexical and syntactic levels. As for the semantic and especially structural levels of adaptation, we assume that information available from parallel sentence pairs is not sufficient and that more global observations and datasets should be exploited.

5 Conclusion and Future Work

In this paper, we introduced the CLEAR corpus with technical and simplified contents in French from the medical field. This kind of corpora is indeed very useful for preparing work on automatic text simplification. The corpus contains texts from three sources: encyclopedia, drug leaflets and summaries of systematic reviews. The source texts are comparable: they propose information on the same topics. The corpus totalizes 16,190 pairs of documents, which corresponds to over 57M word occurrences in the technical part and over 35M word occurrences in the simplified part. A subset of this corpus has been aligned at the sentence level by two annotators with 0.76 inter-annotator agreement. This subset provides 663 pairs of sentences.

In the future, the parallel dataset will be extended automatically further to the design and use of suitable language models. Hence, comparable and parallel datasets will be exploited for designing and testing methods for simplification of medical documents in French. This is an important issue because health-related documents typically contain specialized terminology and notions, which are difficult to be understood by lay people (AMA, 1999; McCray, 2005; Jucks and Bromme, 2007; Kickbusch et al., 2013). In addition to this lexical level, transformations at syntactic level may also be helpful.

The CLEAR corpus with comparable data is available for research and can be found online[11].

6 Acknowledgements

This work was funded by the French National Agency for Research (ANR) as part of the *CLEAR* project (*Communication, Literacy, Education, Accessibility, Readability*), ANR-17-CE19-0016-01. We would like to thank the anonymous reviewers for their comments.

References

AMA. 1999. Health literacy: report of the council on scientific affairs. Ad hoc committee on health literacy for the council on scientific affairs, American Medical Association. *JAMA*, 281(6):552–7.

Ron Artstein and Massimo Poesio. 2008. Inter-coder agreement for computational linguistics. *Computational Linguistics*, 34(4):555–596.

Diana J. Arya, Elfrieda H. Hiebert, and P. David Pearson. 2011. The effects of syntactic and lexical complexity on the comprehension of elementary science texts. *Int Electronic Journal of Elementary Education*, 4(1):107–125.

B Beigman Klebanov, K Knight, and D Marcu. 2004. Text simplification for information-seeking applications. In R Meersman and Z Tari, editors, *On the Move to Meaningful Internet Systems 2004: CoopIS, DOA, and ODBASE*. Springer, LNCS vol 3290, Berlin, Heidelberg.

Or Biran, Samuel Brody, and Noémie Elhadad. 2011. Putting it simply: a context-aware approach to lexical simplification. In *Annual Meeting of the Association for Computational Linguistics*.

Catherine Blake, Julia Kampov, Andreas Orphanides, David West, and Cory Lown. 2007. Query expansion, lexical simplification, and sentence selection strategies for multi-document summarization. In *DUC*.

[11] `http://natalia.grabar.free.fr/resources.php`

Stefan Bott, Horacio Saggion, and Simon Mille. 2014. Text simplification tools for Spanish. In *LREC 2014*, pages 1–7.

Laetitia Brouwers, Delphine Bernhard, Anne-Laure Ligozat, and Thomas Franois. 2012. Simplification syntaxique de phrases pour le français. In *Traitement Automatique des Langues Naturelles (TALN)*, pages 211–224.

Dominique Brunato, Felice Dell'Orletta, Giulia Venturi, and Simonetta Montemagni. 2014. Defining an annotation scheme with a view to automatic text simplification. In *CLICIT*, pages 87–92.

Helena M. Caseli, Tiago F. Pereira, Lucia Specia, Thiago A. S. Pardo, Caroline Gasperin, and Sandra M. Aluisio. 2009. Building a Brazilian Portuguese parallel corpus of original and simplified texts. In *CICLING*, pages 1–12.

R. Chandrasekar, C. Doran, and B. Srinivas. 1996. Motivations and methods for text simplification. In *COLING*, pages 1041–1044.

R Chandrasekar and B Srinivas. 1997. Automatic induction of rules for text simplification. *Knowledge Based Systems*, 10(3):183–190.

Ping Chen, John Rochford, David N. Kennedy, Soussan Djamasbi, Peter Fay, and Will Scott. 2016. Automatic text simplification for people with intellectual disabilities. In *AIST*, pages 1–9.

J Cohen. 1960. A coefficient of agreement for nominal scales. *Educational and Psychological Measurement*, 20(1):37–46.

William Coster and David Kauchak. 2011. Simple English wikipedia: A new text simplification task. In *Annual Meeting of the Association for Computational Linguistics*, pages 665–669.

Walter Daelemans, Anja Höthker, and Erik Tjong Kim Sang. 2004. Automatic sentence simplification for subtitling in Dutch and English. In *LREC*, pages 1045–1048.

Jan De Belder and Marie-Francine Moens. 2010. Text simplification for children. In *Workshop on Accessible Search Systems of SIGIR*, pages 1–8.

N Elhadad and K Sutaria. 2007. Mining a lexicon of technical terms and lay equivalents. In *BioNLP*, pages 49–56.

Pascale Fung and Percy Cheung. 2004. Mining very non-parallel corpora: Parallel sentence and lexicon extraction vie bootstrapping and em. In *Conference on Empirical Methods in Natural Language Processing*, pages 57–63.

Siddhartha Jonnalagadda, Luis Tari, Jörg Hakenberg, Chitta Baral, and Graciela Gonzalez. 2009. Towards effective sentence simplification for automatic processing of biomedical text. In *NAACL HLT 2009*, pages 177–180.

R Jucks and R Bromme. 2007. Choice of words in doctor-patient communication: an analysis of health-related internet sites. *Health Commun*, 21(3):267–77.

I Kickbusch, JM Pelikan, F Apfel, and AD Tsouros. 2013. Health literacy. the solid facts. Technical report, WHO.

Sigrid Klerke and Anders Sgaard. 2012. DSim, a Danish parallel corpus for text simplification. In *LREC*, pages 4015–4018.

JR Landis and GG Koch. 1977. The measurement of observer agreement for categorical data. *Biometrics*, 33:159–174.

Gondy Leroy, David Kauchak, and Obay Mouradi. 2013. A user-study measuring the effects of lexical simplification and coherence enhancement on perceived and actual text difficulty. *Int J Med Inform*, 82(8):717–730.

A Max. 2008. Local rephrasing suggestions for supporting the work of writers. In *GOTAL*, pages 324–335.

A McCray. 2005. Promoting health literacy. *J of Am Med Infor Ass*, 12:152–163.

Rada Mihalcea, Timothy Chklovski, and Adam Kilgarriff. 2004. The SENSEVAL-3 English lexical sample task. In *SENSEVAL-3*, pages 25–28, Barcelona.

Gustavo H. Paetzold and Lucia Specia. 2016. Benchmarking lexical simplification systems. In *LREC*, pages 3074–3080.

Martha Palmer, Hoa Trang Dang, and Christiane Fellbaum. 2007. Making fine-grained and coarse-grained sense distinctions, both manually and automatically. *Natural Language Engineering*, 13(2):137–163.

SE Petersen and M Ostendorf. 2007. Text simplification for language learners: A corpus analysis. In *Speech and Language Technology for Education Workshop (SLaTE)*, pages 69–72.

DL Sackett, WM Rosenberg, JA Gray, RB Haynes, and WS Richardson. 1996. Evidence based medicine: what it is and what it isn't. *BMJ*, 312(7023):71–2.

Advaith Siddharthan. 2006. Syntactic simplification and text cohesion. *Research on Language & Computation*, 4(1):77–109.

Ji Y. Son, Linda B. Smith, and Robert L. Goldstone. 2008. Simplicity and generalization: Short-cutting abstraction in childrens object categorizations. *Cognition*, 108:626–638.

L Specia, SK Jauhar, and R Mihalcea. 2012. Semeval-2012 task 1: English lexical simplification. In **SEM 2012*, pages 347–355.

S Stymne, J Tiedemann, C Hardmeier, and J Nivre. 2013. Statistical machine translation with readability constraints. In *NODALIDA*, pages 1–12.

Sowmya Vajjala and Detmar Meurers. 2015. Readability-based sentence ranking for evaluating text simplification. Technical report, Iowa State University.

Jean Véronis. 1998. A study of polysemy judgments and inter-annotator agreement. In *SENSEVAL-1*, Herstmonceux Castle, England.

D Vickrey and D Koller. 2008. Sentence simplification for semantic role labeling. In *Annual Meeting of the Association for Computational Linguistics-HLT*, pages 344–352.

Sanja Štajner and Maja Popović. 2016. Can text simplification help machine translation? *Baltic J. Modern Computing*, 4(2):230–242.

Tu Thanh Vu, Giang Binh Tran, and Son Bao Pham. 2014. Learning to simplify children stories with limited data. In *Intelligent Information and Database Systems*, pages 31–41.

Chih-Hsuan Wei, Robert Leaman, and Zhiyong Lu. 2014. Simconcept: A hybrid approach for simplifying composite named entities in biomedicine. In *BCB '14*, pages 138–146.

Mark Yatskar, Bo Pang, Cristian Danescu-Niculescu-Mizil, and Lillian Lee. 2010. For the sake of simplicity: Unsupervised extraction of lexical simplifications from Wikipedia. In *NAACL*, pages 365–368.

Z Zhu, D Bernhard, and I Gurevych. 2010. A monolingual tree-based translation model for sentence simplification. In *COLING 2010*, pages 1353–1361.

Study of readability of health documents with eye-tracking approaches

Natalia Grabar
CNRS, UMR 8163, F-59000 Lille, France;
Univ. Lille, UMR 8163 - STL,
F-59000 Lille, France
natalia.grabar@univ-lille.fr

Emmanuel Farce, Laurent Sparrow
Univ. Lille, CNRS,
UMR 9193 - SCALab,
F-59000 Lille, France
emmanuel.farce@univ-lille.fr
laurent.sparrow@univ-lille.fr

Abstract

Medical area is an integral part of our lives due to health concerns, but the availability of medical information does not guarantee its correct understanding by patients. Several studies addressed this issue and pointed out real difficulties in the understanding of health contents by patients. We propose to use eye-tracking methods for studying this issue. For this, original technical and simplified versions of a deidentified clinical document are exploited. Eye-tracking methods permit to follow and to record the gaze of participants and to detect reading indicators such as duration of fixations, regressions and saccades. These indicators are correlated with answers to questionnaires submitted to participants after the reading. Our results indicate that there is statistically significant difference in reading and understanding of original and simplified versions of health documents. These results, in combination with another experiment, permit to propose a typology of medical words which need to be explained or simplified to non-expert readers.

1 Introduction

Medical area is an integral part of our lives due to health concerns and to presence of health information in media and literature. With the evolution of Internet, medical and health information is becoming widely available and accessible online. It has been noticed that, across the world, Internet is positioned at the second place where patients are searching for health information, while the first source of information is still occupied by consultations with medical doctors (Pletneva et al., 2011; Fox, 2011). According to these surveys, up to 24% of the population uses Internet at least once a day to find information on health issues and up to 80% of population is looking for health information on Internet in general. Yet, the availability of medical information does not guarantee its correct understanding by patients. Medical area conveys indeed very specific terminology, like *abdominoplasty, hepatic* or *metatarsophalangeal*. This fact has been stressed by several studies dedicated to poor understanding of health information (McCray, 2005; Patel et al., 2002; Williams et al., 1995; Berland et al., 2001) and to complicated communication between patients and medical staff (Jucks and Bromme, 2007; Tran et al., 2009).

Text complexity is studied in several disciplines, such as linguistics (Iacobini, 2003; Lüdeling et al., 2002), psychology (Bertram et al., 2011; Lüttmann et al., 2011; Bozic et al., 2007; Dohmes et al., 2004; Cain et al., 2009), and NLP (Natural Language Processing) with traditional (Flesch, 1948; Dale and Chall, 1948) and computational (Zeng et al., 2005; Chmielik and Grabar, 2011) approaches. The purpose of our work is to study further the understanding of health documents by non-expert people. We work with data in French. More particularly, we propose to address the reading and understanding of health information through methods and tools provided by eye-tracking. Indeed, study of eye movements during the reading is indicative about the cognitive processes involved. More particularly, text difficulty and readability can be measured with several indicators (Duchowski, 2007; Rayner, 1998; Sparrow et al., 2003; Miellet et al., 2008). Among the eye-tracking indicators, we can mention the following, which are the most exploited in the existing work:

- *Saccades* are rapid movements of eyes during the reading to go from one spot in the

Proceedings of the 1st Workshop on Automatic Text Adaptation (ATA), pages 10–20,
Tilburg, The Netherlands, November 8 2018.

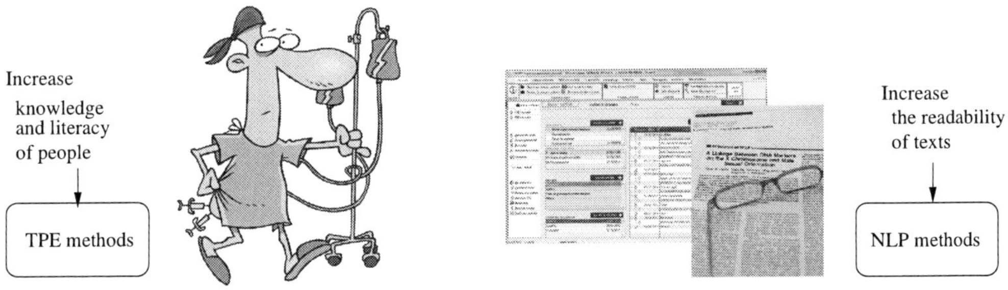

Figure 1: Two aspects related to the understanding of health documents: health literacy of people and readability of documents.

text to another. When the text is easy to read and understand, saccades are longer, and they become shorter when the text is complicated because readers need more time for reading;

- *Fixations* are periods during which the eyes are stable. Fixations correspond to moments when visual information is analyzed. Duration of fixations is increased when the texts are difficult because such texts require longer time for the assimilation of information. Correspondingly, the duration of fixations decreases when the text is easy to read and understand;

- *Regressions* occur when the reader goes back to the text spans already read. When the text is difficult it usually requires more regressions.

Hence, the comparison of eye-tracking parameters (duration of fixations, length of saccades, regressions, etc.) recorded during the reading of texts permits to evaluate with more precision difficulties and blocking points of readers.

According to our hypotheses, reading of complex texts and unknown terms condition our attention and the movements of our eyes present then typical and observable patterns. Such indicators can be directly correlated with difficulties occurring during the text reading and understanding: for instance, when a text contains technical terms, the reading speed and fixations are longer, and require more time for the assimilation. We propose to exploit the findings from the eye-tracking experiments for the detection of blocking reading points in medical texts and for providing a typology of medical words for which reading and understanding may present some difficulties. This typology is also supported by another set of experiments performed with medical terms in French. One issue is that these medical words and terms should be simplified or explained to laypeople and patients for making better their understanding of the medical contents.

Eye-tracking and its indicators are exploited in several contexts for the detection of text spans that attract or block the eye movements and the reading, such as: relation between speech and eye movements, when participants are looking at picture segments which correspond to the sentences they are hearing (Cooper, 1974; Tanenhaus et al., 1995; Wendt et al., 2014); reading of texts in first and second languages (Altarriba et al., 1996; Bisson et al., 2014); reading of texts by dyslexic people (Rubino and Minden, 1973; Elterman et al., 1980; Nilsson Benfatto et al., 2016) and autists (Yaneva et al., 2015); processing of syntactic structures (Frenck-Mestre and Pynte, 1997; Clifton and Staub, 2011; Trueswell et al., 1994; Singh et al., 2016); detection and processing of errors (Keating, 2009); evaluation of text complexity during the translation (Sharmin et al., 2008) and language acquisition (Balakrishna, 2015).

Usually, in relation with understanding of texts, two closely related aspects are distinguished (Figure 1):

1. On one side, patients have a given level of literacy and of health literacy, when situated in the health area. This aspect is researched by Therapeutic Patient Education (TPE), which purpose is to diagnose and to improve the health literacy of patients (Golay et al., 2007; Pélicand et al., 2009; Glasgow et al., 2012). Such actions are usually done by experts in patient education (specialized medical doctors, speech therapists, sociologists, psychologists, nurses...);

EXAM: SONOGRAPHY OF HANDS AND FEET
REASON: Arthralgia
Hands: Tenosynovitis and arthrosynovitis cannot be observed.
Forefoot: Interesting reorganization of the first metatarsophalangeal can be seen, in relation with the history of surgery of hallux valgus.
Absence of arthrosynovitis at the level of metatarsophalangeal articulations.

EXAM: SONOGRAPHY OF HANDS AND FEET
REASON: Pain in articulations
Hands: Inflammation of tendons or of articulation membrane cannot be observed.
Forefoot: Interesting reorganization of the first foot articulations can be seen, in relation with the history of surgery of foot deformation.
Absence of inflammation of the membrane at the level of foot articulations.

Figure 2: Translated examples with original (upper) and simplified (lower) texts.

2. On the other side, health documents show a given readability level and can be more or less difficult to read and to understand. Here, the purpose is to diagnose the difficulty of information and to make this information more easily accessible for laypeople. Typically, this process is addressed by researchers in NLP for the readability diagnosis and for the text simplification (Biran et al., 2011; Brouwers et al., 2012; Glavas and Stajner, 2015).

Our work is related to the second aspect: diagnosis of text readability.

In what follows, we first present the material used (Section 2) and the protocol of the approach (Section 3) to reach the objectives. Section 4 is dedicated to the description and discussion of the results obtained, and Section 5 draws the conclusion and proposes some issues for the future work. All experiments are performed with the French-language data.

2 Material

Two short excerpts of deidentified clinical documents are used: summary discharge in cardiology and radiology report of feet and hands. These texts are used in two versions: original (technical) and manually simplified (see Figure 2). Due to the experimental setting of eye-tracking experiments, the texts used are short: 48 words in text_1 and 112 words text_2. For the simplification, we use automatically built resources (Grabar and Hamon, 2014; Antoine and Grabar, 2016), which provide pairs of equivalent terms such as {*myocard*; *heart muscle*}, {*desmorrhexy*; *rupture of ligaments*}, and pairs of hyperonyms such as {*metatarsophalangeal*→*foot*}. Synonyms and paraphrases are used in priority, and hyperonyms are used when synonyms and paraphrases are not available. The simplification is typically done for words and terms which have been judged as non-understandable in previous research, for which almost 30,000 medical words from the UMLS (Lindberg et al., 1993) and Snomed International (Côté, 1996) terms have been manually categorized as understandable or non-understandable (Grabar and Hamon, 2016). Overall, the text_1 has undergone seven modifications, and the text_2 ten modifications. After the simplification, text_1 contains 65 words and text_2 82 words. As a matter of fact, text_1 has become longer because its original version contains several compoundings which simplification requires paraphrasing with several words.

These texts are used to build two testsets, in which the order of technical and simplified texts varies:

- testset_1: original text_1 and simplified text_2,
- testset_2: simplified text_1 and original text_2.

Figure 2 presents the English translation of the text_1 in the original and simplified versions.

3 Approach

We first describe the inclusion criteria of this study, and then the protocol of the eye-tracking experiments, and the analysis of the obtained data (Sections 3.1 to 3.3).

3.1 Inclusion Criteria

50 participants are recruited and each testset is read by 25 of them, so that statistical significance

between original and simplified versions can be computed. Can be included in the study:

1. undergraduate students from different disciplines (psychology, linguistics, history, communication studies...). Medical and paramedical students are excluded. Usually, 5 levels of literacy are distinguished (Bernèche and Perron, 2006):
   - levels 1 and 2 correspond to persons who have serious difficulties in reading, understanding and assimilation of information;
   - level 3 gathers people who usually have standard readability and literacy level. They are fluent in reading and can understand general language purposes;
   - levels 4 and 5 correspond to persons who show the capacity to read, understand and make complex deductions, which is often specific to persons with high school education.

   Undergraduate students are usually associated with the third level of literacy, and are representative of the average citizens (Bernèche and Perron, 2006);
2. people without chronic disorders because in that case they may be familiar with medical terminology;
3. people without dyslexia because they have difficulties with reading, which are not specifically due to the reading of specialized texts, such as aimed in our study;
4. people with French as first language, which provide the common basis for all participants and guarantees that difficulties in reading and understanding are not due to other causes than specificity of the medical field.

3.2 Eye-tracking Protocol

The proposed approach is based on exploitation of eye-tracking, which purpose is to measure the fluidity of reading with objective measures like the number of saccades, the duration of saccades, the number of fixations, the duration of the first fixation, or the regressions (Sparrow et al., 2003; Miellet et al., 2008). These indicators typically permit to detect text zones which obstruct the reading and the understanding, as the two of them are related. The texts are presented on a display, and specific camera (EyeLink 1000) permits to capture eye movements and to relate them with the text.

> *The heart is supplied in blood by coronary arteries which are fed by another artery: the aorta. When the diameter of coronary arteries is reduced because of progressive formation of fat patches, cardiac muscle is no more supplied in oxygen and nutrients: it is suffering. If the artery is blocked completely, infarctus may be close... Bypass and stent have the same purpose: restore normal blood flow.*

Figure 3: Translation of the control text (step 4).

After the presentation of the objectives of the study, each participant goes though:

1. parameterizing of the eye-tracking camera,
2. reading of a general text for training,
3. reading of the testset_1 or of the testset_2, with medical texts in original and simplified versions,
4. reading of the control text with lay medical contents (Figure 3).
5. After the reading of each text, the participant has to answer multiple choice questionnaires (two questions per text) to control the understanding of these texts. On the text_1, these two questions are asked:
   - *The sonography is done for: (1) shoulder, (2) hands and feet, (3) I do not know*
   - *Which inflammations are looked for: (1) articulations only, (2) articulations and tendons, (3) I do not know*

   On the text_2, these two questions are asked:
   - *The patient has problems: (1) cardiac, (2) cerebral, (3) I do not know*
   - *The patient is treated with: (1) surgery, (2) genetically, (3) I do not know*

   On the control text, these two questions are asked:
   - *The arteries can be damaged with: (1) fat patches, (2) calcium patches, (3) I do not know*

	Text$_1$						Text$_2$					
	O	*S*	*std.*	*p*	*dof*	*t-test*	*O*	*S*	*std.*	*p*	*dof*	*t-test*
TRN	60,55	63,63	-3,08	0,23	45,00	1,22	62,73	59,67	3,06	0,22	45,00	1,24
CRL	58,88	62,06	-3,19	0,22	45,00	1,25	61,04	57,84	3,20	0,21	45,00	1,29
DFF	227,41	215,75	11,66	0,11	45,00	1,65	214,73	214,69	0,04	0,50	45,00	0,68
TNF	587,61	370,48	217,14	**0,00**	45,00	7,38	395,71	372,22	23,49	0,16	45,00	1,43
AMP	3,50	3,80	-0,30	**0,02**	45,00	2,44	3,33	3,82	-0,49	**0,00**	45,00	5,38
REG	27,26	21,21	6,06	**0,05**	45,00	2,05	21,47	19,30	2,18	0,24	45,00	1,18
MCQ	1304,35	869,57	434,78	**0,02**	21,00	2,08	602,77	538,95	63,82	**0,00**	21,00	2,08

Table 1: Results for the two versions of the texts (original O and simplified S) and their statistical analysis. The indicators are the following: training text *TRN* and control text *CRL*; duration of the first fixation *DFF*, total number of fixations *TNF*, amplitude of saccades *AMP*, number of regressions *REG*; answers to questions *MCQ*. Statistically significant p is marked with bold characters.

- *When the artery is blocked, there is risk of: (1) headaches, (2) infarctus, (3) I do not know*

6. At the end, if desired, the results recorded further to his reading are presented and explained to the participant.

Overall the experiment lasts for 15 to 20 minutes.

3.3 Analysis of Eye-tracking Data

The data collected during the eye-tracking experiments are analyzed with several statistical measures, such as *t test*, statistical significance, degree of freedom (Walker, 1940) and standard deviation. The objective is to assess the difference of indicators when reading original and simplified versions of texts. We expect that the simplified version of texts is read more easily, *e.g.* with short fixations, long saccades and no regressions.

4 Results and Discussion

We first present the results obtained from the presented eye-tracking experience (Section 4.1) and discuss them, we then indicate some advantages of using the eye-tracking methodology (Section 4.2) and some known limitations (Section 4.3), and propose a typology of words that may present reading difficulties in medical texts (Section 4.4).

4.1 Results from the Eye-tracking Protocol

In Figure 4, we present an example of reading of the text$_1$: the original (upper graphics) and simplified (lower graphics) versions. In Figure 5, we present another example obtained while reading the text$_2$ in original and simplified versions. On these Figures, we can easily observe differences in reading of original and simplified versions.

In Table 1, we present the average reading indicators for the two tested versions (original O and simplified S) and their statistical analysis: the reading time for the original O and the simplified S versions, the standard deviation $sdt.$, the p-value p, the degree of freedom dof, and the $t - test$ value. These results are provided for the text$_1$ and the text$_2$, and for each indicator studied. The results indicate that:

- *Reading time of the training (TRN) and control (CRL) texts.* No statistical difference is observed with the reading time of the training and control texts. This indicates that the participants have the same reading capacity and that their reading results on medical texts are comparable. This is a good observation which points out that further results are comparable;

- *Duration of the first fixation (DFF).* No difference is observed for the duration of the first fixation. This indicates that reading of the two versions of texts starts in a similar way, that the participants do not anticipate on the nature of the texts (original or simplified), and again that further results are comparable;

- *Total number of fixations (TNF).* Statistically significant difference is observed for the total duration of fixations for the text$_1$: on the original version the fixations are more frequent. This can be observed on Figure 4: on the original (upper) text, the blue dots are more frequent than on the simplified (lower)

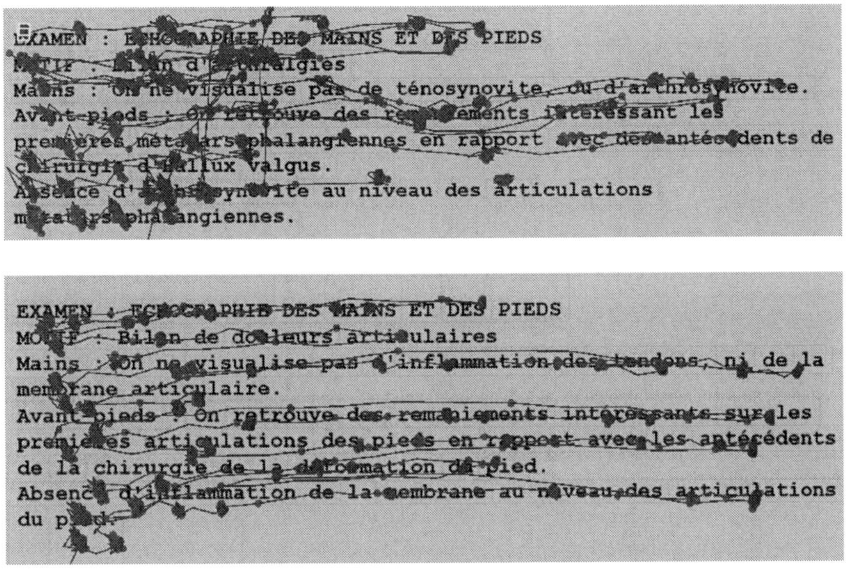

Figure 4: Examples of reading of original (upper) and simplified (lower) versions of $texts_1$.

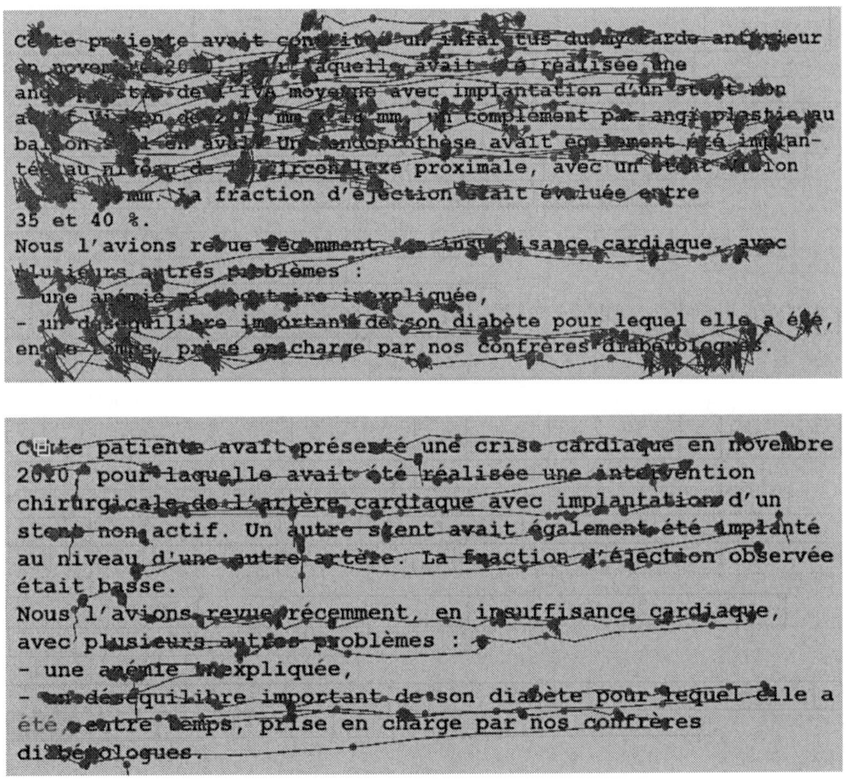

Figure 5: Examples of reading of original (upper) and simplified (lower) versions of $texts_2$.

text. For instance, in the original text, compound words like *arthralgia*, *arthrosynovitis* or *metatarsophalangeal* can require several fixations, which may correspond to the syllables of these words. Besides, this kind of terms also show longer fixations by the participants (the dots are larger). The technical version of the $text_2$ does not require that many fixations, may be due to the fact that it does not contain compounds;

- *Amplitude of saccades (AMP).* The simplification of the texts causes the increasing of the amplitude of saccades. As indicated in Table 1, this indicator is statistically significant for the $text_1$ and the $text_2$. This means that simplification decreases the reading difficulty. Hence, on Figures 4 and 5, the horizontal blue lines are shorter on the original texts than on the simplified texts;

- *Regressions (REG).* The number of regressions is statistically important for the $text_1$ but not for the $text_2$. This suggests that the reading of the simplified version of the $text_1$ is more fluent. This can also be observed on Figure 4: on the original text, we can see vertical blue lines;

- *Answers to the questionnaires (MCQ).* The analysis of the answers to questions indicates that the understanding of the simplified version is always better for the simplified versions than for the technical versions. The difference is statistically significant for the two texts. Hence, we obtain 54% of correct answers for the original versions and up to 81% of correct answers for the simplified versions.

On the whole, we can observe that the simplification of text improves all the reading indicators: (1) the total duration of fixations is lesser, (2) the amplitude of saccades is bigger, and (3) the regressions are less frequent. These results provide coherent and stable reading indicators and reading patterns specific to the technical original and the simplified versions of the medical texts. These results also indicate that the simplification of health documents is an efficient way to improve their reading and understanding by non-expert readers. As indicated all indicators show statistically significant differences on the $text_1$ and some of them are also statistically significant on the $text_2$. On both texts, correct answers to questions are correlated with the text difficulty.

4.2 Advantages of Eye-tracking

The eye-tracking technology offers several advantages which can be exploited in different tasks, such as those presented in Section 1. We present here some of these advantages, which have been very useful in our experiments:

- Several indicators on the reading process can be computed and exploited. Typically, these indicators are: the number and duration of fixations, the amplitude of saccades, the number of regressions;

- The eye-tracking indicators are objective: they are non-conscious and non-controlled by people. They are directly impacted by the individual reading habits acquired during the scholar and family learning;

- The eye-tracking indicators can be correlated with other types of information such as understanding of texts, social and professional status of participants, etc.;

- During the reading, the words and terms are considered within their contexts and the global perception of texts is usually expected from participants.

4.3 Limitations of Eye-tracking

Yet, the eye-tracking technology presents some known limitations, which are usually taken into account in experiments (Duchowski, 2007):

- Eye-tracking camera permits to detect and to record the gaze of the participants. The common hypothesis is that the gaze is correlated with the attention of participants, while in reality attention can also be oriented on objects which are located on peripheral areas of the gaze. Human vision system is indeed very sophisticated and currently it is not fully decoded yet. This is one of the known limitations of the eye-tracking methodology and it requires that the two possibilities are accepted: the gaze matches with the explicit attention of participants or does not match. In our case, with the reading of short medical texts, the requirement to answer questions after the reading, and the absence of distractors (the tests have been performed in experimental lab conditions), we assume that the attention of readers matches with their gaze;

- With some participants, due to their physiological specificities (long eyelashes, make-up, heavy eyelids...), it can be complicated to parameter the eye-tracking camera, and to track and record the eye movements. This can lead to loss of data or to wrong superposition of gaze recording on the texts. Nevertheless, when the data are exploitable, there is no impact on the reading indicators;
- Similarly, eyeglasses and contact lenses can be problematic for the tracking of the pupil and of its movements;
- For a given text or picture, the attention and the gaze of participants vary according to the task and the questions they are being asked. In our experiment, all the participants had to do the same task which consisted in text reading and answering to questions. The instructions have been presented clearly at the beginning of the test and before each reading;
- Eye-tracking cameras also have some limitations: (1) they work with a given frequency (60 Hz) and some eye movements can be missed and not recorded; (2) the recorded signal is cleaned up, such as with blinking or some peripheral eye movements, which can also remove some important eye movements;
- Due to the test requirements, the tests can be performed only with short texts which can be easily displayed and read by all participants from a computer screen. This means that several tests and experiments are necessary to cover more texts and to increase their diversity.

4.4 Typology of difficulties

The results obtained from the presented experiments permit to propose a typology of some medical words and terms that may present reading and understanding difficulties to laypeople. Notice that this typology is confirmed and completed by larger experiments done with medical terminologies in French: almost 30,000 medical words from the UMLS (Lindberg et al., 1993) and Snomed International (Côté, 1996) in French. These terms have been manually categorized as understandable or non-understandable (Grabar and Hamon, 2016).

The complete proposed typology contains the following types of linguistic units:

- abbreviations (*IVA, NIHSS, OAP, NaCl, VNI, OG, VG, PAPS, j, bat, cp*);
- borrowings from Latin or English (*stent, Hallux valgus*);
- proper names (*Gougerot, Sjögren, Bentall, Glasgow, Babinski, Barthel, Cockcroft*);
- drug names (*CALCIPARINE*);
- neoclassical compounds meaning disorders, procedures or treatments (*endoprothesis, pseudohémophilie, sclérodermie, hydrolase, tympanectomie, arthrodèse, synesthésie*);
- human anatomy (*metatarsophalangeal, microcytic, cloacal, pubovaginal, nasopharyngé, mitral, antre, inguinal, strontium, érythème, maxillo-facial, mésentère*);
- lab test results with numeral values and their interpretation.

Such units are very frequent in different types of medical texts and potentially present an important understanding difficulty. We assume that such words and terms must be explained or simplified to laypeople to guarantee a more correct understanding of medical texts by them. This task can be typically addressed during the automatic text simplification or adaptation.

Due to the experimental set-up, only two short excerpts from medical texts have been used (160 words in technical versions and 147 words in simplified versions, in total). Currently, it is difficult to link the typology classes to the eye-tracking indicators. Nevertheless, we can present here some first observations:

- *Abbreviations.* The $text_2$ contains one abbreviation (*IVA*), which required longer fixations of the participants;
- *Borrowings.* The $text_1$ contains one borrowing from Latin (*Hallux valgus*), which was read normally by participants. One possible explanation collected from participants is that uppercased *H* in *Hallux valgus* associated this term with a proper name;

- *Proper names.* No real proper names occur in the two texts;
- *Drug names.* No drug names occur in the two texts;
- *Neoclassical compounds.* The tested texts, and especially the $text_1$, contain several compounds. As already indicated above, compounds require several fixations and these fixations are longer. Compounds may also require regressions;
- *Human anatomy.* Several terms related to human anatomy occur in the two texts. Excepting very frequent terms (like *foot* or *hand*), human anatomy terms usually require several fixations and these fixations are longer;
- *Numeral values.* The $text_2$ contains several numerical values. These values require longer fixations and also regressions.

These are just first raw observations obtained from two small medical texts in French.

5 Conclusion and Future Work

We proposed an experiment on studying the effect of simplification of medical texts addressed through the use of eye-tracking methods. In this way, we can obtain several objective reading indicators, such as duration of fixations, amplitude of saccades and regressions. The collected indicators are then compared between the original and simplified versions of a given text with statistical measures to analyze if there is statistically significant differences when reading technical and simplified medical contents. Then, two understanding questions (multiple choice questionnaires) are asked to the participants after the reading of each text.

The results obtained indicate that reading of the two versions of the texts, original and simplified, provide coherent and stable reading patterns. For instance, when reading the simplified version, the fixations are shorter, the saccades are longer and the regressions absent or infrequent. Additionally, the analysis of the answers to questions indicates that the understanding of the simplified version is better: the number of correct answers varies between 54% for the original text and up to 81% for the simplified text. This also indicates that medical texts can be efficiently simplified in order to obtain their better understanding by non-expert persons.

These tests, together with data obtained from previous experiments, also permitted to propose a typology of medical words and terms that may present blocking points and difficulties with understanding. This typology include abbreviations, borrowed words, proper names, drug names, compounds, terms related to human anatomy and numbers. We assume that these kinds of terms should be simplified for a better understanding of medical texts by patients. Our first results permitted to associate some of these classes with eye-tracking indicators. For instance, compounds require more fixations and these fixations are longer. They may also require regressions.

We have several directions for future research. For instance, it would be interesting to study the relation between the text length and its readability and understanding. The hypothesis is that longer texts, even if they are simpler, may yet present reading and understanding difficulties. The impact of other factors (such as definitions, favorable contexts, pictures) can also be studied. Due to the experimental constraints, only short excepts of texts are used. For this reasons, it may be interesting to perform additional tests with a greater variety of text types and of simplification versions. Terms related to the proposed typology will be addressed in other works in order to perform their automatic explanation or simplification. In order to address different levels of literacy, different principles may be used when performing the simplification. These principes and the corresponding rules will be defined and tested in future work. Besides, like with manual simplification, the efficiency of automatic simplification methods can also be tested and evaluated using eye-tracking protocols.

6 Acknowledgements

This work was funded by the French National Agency for Research (ANR) as part of the *CLEAR* project (*Communication, Literacy, Education, Accessibility, Readability*), ANR-17-CE19-0016-01. The excerpts of the texts used have been obtained during the RAVEL project funded by the French National Agency for Research (ANR) and the DGA, under grant Tecsan ANR-11-TECS-012.

We would like to thank again the participants in the eye-tracking study. Also, we would like to thank the anonymous reviewers for their helpful comments.

References

J Altarriba, J Kroll, A Sholl, and K Rayner. 1996. The influence of lexical and conceptual constraints on reading mixed-language sentences: Evidence from eye fixations and naming times. *Memory and Cognition*, 24:477–92.

E Antoine and N Grabar. 2016. Exploitation de reformulations pour l'acquisition d'un vocabulaire expert/non expert. In *Traitement Automatique des Langues Naturelles (TALN)*.

SV Balakrishna. 2015. *Analyzing Text Complexity and Text Simplification: Connecting Linguistics, Processing and Educational Applications*. Thèse de doctorat, Eberhard Karls Universität Tübingen, Tübingen, Germany.

GK Berland, MN Elliott, LS Morales, JI Algazy, RL Kravitz, MS Broder, DE Kanouse, JA Munoz, JA Puyol, and M Lara et al. 2001. Health information on the Internet. Accessibility, quality, and readability in english ans spanish. *JAMA*, 285(20):2612–2621.

Francine Bernèche and Bertrand Perron. 2006. Développer nos compétences en littératie: un défi porteur d'avenir. Enquête internationale sur l'alphabétisation et les compétences des adultes. Technical report, Institut de la statistique du Québec, Canada.

Raymond Bertram, Victor Kuperman, Harald R Baayen, and Jukka Hyönä. 2011. The hyphen as a segmentation cue in triconstituent compound processing: Its getting better all the time. *Scandinavian Journal of Psychology*, 52(6):530–544.

Or Biran, Samuel Brody, and Noémie Elhadad. 2011. Putting it simply: a context-aware approach to lexical simplification. In *Annual Meeting of the Association for Computational Linguistics*.

MJ Bisson, W Van Heuven, K Conklin, and R Tunney. 2014. Processing of native and foreign language subtitles in films: An eye-tracking study. *Applied Psycholinguistics*, 35:399–418.

Mirjana Bozic, William D. Marslen-Wilson, Emmanuel A. Stamatakis, Matthew H. Davis, and Lorraine K. Tyler. 2007. Differentiating morphology, form, and meaning: Neural correlates of morphological complexity. *Journal of Cognitive Neuroscience*, 19(9):1464–1475.

Laetitia Brouwers, Delphine Bernhard, Anne-Laure Ligozat, and Thomas François. 2012. Simplification syntaxique de phrases pour le français. In *Traitement Automatique des Langues Naturelles (TALN)*, pages 211–224.

Kate Cain, Andrea S. Towse, and Rachael S. Knight. 2009. The development of idiom comprehension: An investigation of semantic and contextual processing skills. *Journal of Experimental Child Psychology*, 102(3):280–298.

J Chmielik and N Grabar. 2011. Détection de la spécialisation scientifique et technique des documents biomédicaux grâce aux informations morphologiques. *TAL*, 51(2):151–179.

C Clifton and A Staub. 2011. Syntactic influences on eye movements in reading. In S Liversedge, I Gilchrist, and S Everling, editors, *The Oxford handbook of eye movements*, pages 895–909. Oxford University Press.

RM Cooper. 1974. The control of eye fixation by the meaning of spoken language: A new methodology for the real-time investigation of speech perception, memory, and language processing. *Cognitive Psychol*, 6:84–107.

RA Côté. 1996. *Répertoire d'anatomopathologie de la SNOMED internationale, v3.4*. Université de Sherbrooke, Sherbrooke, Québec.

E Dale and JS Chall. 1948. A formula for predicting readability. *Educational research bulletin*, 27:11–20.

Petra Dohmes, Pienie Zwitserlood, and Jens Bölte. 2004. The impact of semantic transparency of morphologically complex words on picture naming. *Brain and Language*, 90(1-3):203–212.

Andrew Duchowski. 2007. *Eye Tracking Methodology. Theory and practice*. Springer, London, UK.

RD Elterman, LA Abel, RB Daroff, LF DellOsso, and JL Bornstein. 1980. Eye movement patterns in dyslexic children. *J Learn Disabil*, 13:16–21.

R Flesch. 1948. A new readability yardstick. *Journ Appl Psychol*, 23:221–233.

Susannah Fox. 2011. Health topics. 80% of Internet users look for health information online. Technical report, Pew Internet & American Life Project, Washington DC.

C Frenck-Mestre and J Pynte. 1997. Syntactic ambiguity resolution while reading in a second and native languages. *The Quarterly Journal of Experimental Psychology*, 50(1):119–48.

Russell E. Glasgow, Deanna Kurz, Diane King, Jennifer M. Dickman, Andrew J. Faber, Eve Halterman, Tim Woolley, Deborah J. Toobert, and Lisa A. Strycker et al. 2012. Twelve-month outcomes of an Internet-based diabetes self-management support program. *Patient Education and Communication*, 87(1):81–92.

Goran Glavas and Sanja Stajner. 2015. Simplifying lexical simplification: Do we need simplified corpora? In *ACL-COLING*, pages 63–68.

A. Golay, G. Lagger, and A. Giordan. 2007. Motivating patient with chronic diseases. *Journ of Med and the Person*, 5(2):57–63.

Natalia Grabar and Thierry Hamon. 2014. Automatic extraction of layman names for technical medical terms. In *ICHI 2014*, Pavia, Italy.

Natalia Grabar and Thierry Hamon. 2016. A large rated lexicon with French medical words. In *LREC (Language Resources and Evaluation Conference)*, pages 1–12.

C Iacobini. 2003. Composizione con elementi neoclassici. In Maria Grossmann and Franz Rainer, editors, *La formazione delle parole in italiano*, pages 69–96. Walter de Gruyter.

R Jucks and R Bromme. 2007. Choice of words in doctor-patient communication: an analysis of health-related internet sites. *Health Commun*, 21(3):267–77.

G Keating. 2009. Sensitivity to violations of gender agreement in native and non-native Spanish: An eye-movement investigation. *Language Learning*, 59:503–35.

DA Lindberg, BL Humphreys, and AT McCray. 1993. The Unified Medical Language System. *Methods Inf Med*, 32(4):281–291.

A Lüdeling, T Schmidt, and S Kiokpasoglou. 2002. Neoclassical word formation in German. *Yearbook of Morphology*, pages 253–283.

Heidi Lüttmann, Pienie Zwitserlood, and Jens Bölte. 2011. Sharing morphemes without sharing meaning: Production and comprehension of German verbs in the context of morphological relatives. *Canadian Journal of Experimental Psychology/Revue canadienne de psychologie exprimentale*, 65(3):173–191.

A McCray. 2005. Promoting health literacy. *J of Am Med Infor Ass*, 12:152–163.

S Miellet, L Sparrow, and S Sereno. 2008. The effects of frequency and predictability in French: An evaluation of the E-Z Reader model. *Psychonomic Bulletin & Review*, 14:762–769.

M Nilsson Benfatto, G qvist Seimyr, J Ygge, T Pansell, A Rydberg, and C Jacobson. 2016. Screening for dyslexia using eye tracking during reading. *PLoS ONE*, 11(12):e0165508.

V Patel, T Branch, and J Arocha. 2002. Errors in interpreting quantities as procedures : The case of pharmaceutical labels. *Int Journ Med Inform*, 65(3):193–211.

J Pélicand, C Fournier, and I Aujoulat. 2009. Observance, auto-soin(s), empowerment, autonomie: quatre termes pour questionner les enjeux de l'éducation du patient dans la relation de soins. *ADSP*, 66:21–23.

N Pletneva, A Vargas, and C Boyer. 2011. How do general public search online health information? Technical report, Health On the Net Foundation.

K Rayner. 1998. Eye movements in reading and information processing: 20 years of research. *Psychological bulletin*, 124(3):372–373.

CA Rubino and HA Minden. 1973. Analysis of eye-movements in children with reading disability. *Cortex*, 9:217–220.

S Sharmin, O Spakov, KJ Rih, and AL Jakobsen. 2008. Effects of time pressure and text complexity on translators fixations. In *ETNA*, pages 123–126.

AD Singh, P Mehta, S Husain, and R Rajkumar. 2016. Quantifying sentence complexity based on eye-tracking measures. In *Workshop on Computational Linguistics for Linguistic Complexity*, pages 202–212.

Laurent Sparrow, S Miellet, and Yann Coello. 2003. The effects of frequency and predictability on eye fixations in reading: An evaluation of the E-Z reader model. *Behavioral and Brain Sciences*, 26:503–505.

MK Tanenhaus, MJ Spivey-Knowiton, KM Eberharda, and JC Sedivy. 1995. Integration of visual and linguistic information in spoken language comprehension. *Science*, 268:1632–1634.

TM Tran, H Chekroud, P Thiery, and A Julienne. 2009. Internet et soins : un tiers invisible dans la relation médecine/patient ? *Ethica Clinica*, 53:34–43.

J Trueswell, M Tanenhaus, and S Garnsey. 1994. Semantic influences on parsing: Use of thematic role information in syntactic ambiguity resolution. *Journal of Memory and Language*, 33:285–318.

HM Walker. 1940. Degrees of freedom. *Journal of Educational Psychology*, 31(4):253–269.

D Wendt, T Brand, and B Kollmeier. 2014. An eye-tracking paradigm for analyzing the processing time of sentences with different linguistic complexities. *PLoS ONE*, 9(6):e100186.

MV Williams, RM Parker, DW Baker, NS Parikh, K Pitkin, WC Coates, and JR Nurss. 1995. Inadequate functional health literacy among patients at two public hospitals. *JAMA*, 274(21):1677–1682.

V Yaneva, I Temnikova, and R Mitkov. 2015. Accessible texts for autism: An eye-tracking study. In *Int ACM SIGACCESS Conference on Computers & Accessibility*, pages 49–57.

Qing T Zeng, Tony Tse, Jon Crowell, Guy Divita, Laura Roth, and Allen C Browne. 2005. Identifying consumer-friendly display (CFD) names for health concepts. In *Ann Symp Am Med Inform Assoc (AMIA)*, pages 859–63.

Assisted Lexical Simplification for French Native Children with Reading Difficulties

Firas Hmida[1]
Aix-Marseille Univ.
LPL UMR 7309
Aix-en-Pce, France

Mokhtar B. Billami[1]
Aix-Marseille Univ.
LIS UMR 7020
Marseille, France

Thomas François[2]
UCLouvain
CENTAL/IL&C
Louvain-la-Neuve, Belgium

Núria Gala[1]
Aix-Marseille Univ.
LPL UMR 7309
Aix-en-Pce, France

firstname.lastname@{[1]univ-amu.fr,[2]uclouvain.be}

Abstract

For poor-readers and dyslexic children, reading is often a pitfall to social integration and academic progress. The school support of these children usually requires adapted texts, specialised glossaries and dedicated management tools. In this paper, we propose a method which exploits French lexical resources to automatically simplify words in order to provide adapted texts. Despite the difficulty of the task, the conducted evaluations show that the proposed methodology yields better results than the state of the art word2vec techniques for lexical simplification.

1 Introduction

Learning to read is a complex and lengthy process leading to a fundamental skill which is crucial for academic, professional and personal success. Yet, according to the Progress in International Reading Literacy (PIRLS[1]) 2001, the overall performances of French young readers is gradually decreasing from evaluation to evaluation: 39% of the students are in difficulty at the end of primary school according to the study carried by the Cycle of Disciplinary Evaluations Performed on Samples[2]. Statistically, every year, 2 to 5 children in a classroom present a specific language impairment (from poor-reading to dyslexia, with a large variability). Ziegler et al. (2003) show that the problems of comprehension among children with reading difficulties are mostly due to the difficulties in decoding words in order to recognise them. In other words, these children do not suffer from oral comprehension problems. However, when it comes to reading a text, it turns out that all their efforts are so focused on decoding that they exhaust their cognitive capacity. Out of hand, they get tired, give up reading and lose the meaning of what they have already read.

In this context, scholars have found it valuable to control the reading difficulty of pedagogical materials using readability formulae (DuBay, 2004). Text readability can be defined as the ease with which a reader can read and understand a text. Readability assessment techniques enable a better association between texts and readers, which tends to increase the benefits of reading practices. However, even if readability formulae are useful to find appropriate texts for a given level of reading proficiency, they do not allow to adapt a given text to a specific reader, as is generally needed for poor readers or readers with dyslexia.

More recently, Natural Language Processing (NLP) techniques have allowed the development of more efficient tools to support reading. Among them are advanced readability models (Collins-Thompson, 2014) that automatically assess the readability of a text from a larger number of text characteristics. Another promising area is automated text simplification (ATS), which aims to automatically substitute complex linguistic phenomena in texts by simpler equivalents while keeping the meaning preserved as much as possible. ATS is generally described as involving two sub-tasks (Saggion, 2017): syntactic simplification and lexical simplification (LS). In this paper, we will be concerned with the second one, because, as far as poor and dyslexic readers are concerned, automatic lexical simplification is a first and crucial step in order to simplify a text for this population.

As it has been highlighted in the literature, long and less frequent words are especially difficult for poor readers (Ziegler et al., 2003; Spinelli et al.,

[1]https://timssandpirls.bc.edu/pirls2001i/pdf/p1_IR_book.pdf

[2]Cycle des Évaluations Disciplinaires Réalisées sur Échantillons (CEDRE).

Proceedings of the 1st Workshop on Automatic Text Adaptation (ATA), pages 21–28,
Tilburg, The Netherlands, November 8 2018.

2005). Gala and Ziegler (2016) also identified that, for French children with dyslexia, inconsistent words as far as the grapheme-phoneme relation is concerned (different length of the number of letters and phonemes in a word) contribute to the difficulty in reading.

In this paper, we address the challenging task of LS, which has not yet been systematically investigated for French. We compare two approaches: the first one is based on the exploitation of a lexical resource, ReSyf[3] (Billami et al., 2018), which contains disambiguated ranked synonyms in French; the second one is based on word embedding and draws from Glavaš and Štajner (2015). Although previous studies have prioritised statistical methods over the use of resources to acquire synonyms, we are not aware of a previous study having compared statistical models with a **disambiguated** synonym resource. We believe that this property could significantly enhance the selection of relevant candidates for substitution in a given context. Another property of ReSyf is that synonyms have already been ranked by reading difficulty using Billami et al. (2018) method.

The paper is organised as follows: Section 2 presents existing methods for LS. Section 3 describes our method and Section 4 discusses on the results. Some concluding remarks are to be found at the end, along with future work.

2 State of the Art

Text simplification refers to the process of transforming a text into an equivalent which is easier to read and to understand than the original, while preserving, in essence, the original content (Bott et al., 2012). Lexical simplification (LS) is dedicated to the substitution of complex words by simpler synonyms. Complex words are here considered as mono-lexical units which are difficult to read (i.e. decode), especially for poor and dyslexic readers. LS aims to provide, for a complex word in a text, a simpler substitute making this text more accessible to the reader (the meaning and the syntactic structure of the text is as far as possible preserved).

Previous works have shown the contribution of LS to make texts more accessible to different audiences: people with dyslexia (Rello et al., 2013a,c,b), with aphasia (Carroll et al., 1998; Devlin, 1999), illiterate and poor readers (Aluísio et al., 2010) to name a few. Text simplification systems exist for various languages, for example: English (Carroll et al., 1998; Horn et al., 2014; Glavaš and Štajner, 2015; Paetzold and Specia, 2017), Spanish (Bott et al., 2012; Rello et al., 2013a), Swedish (Keskisärkkä, 2012), and Portuguese (Aluísio and Gasperin, 2010). However, to our knowledge, there is no full-fledged ATS system for French available, although some authors have investigated related aspects (i.e. simplified writing for language-impaired readers (Max, 2006), French readability for French as a Foreign Language (FFL) (François and Fairon, 2012), syntactic simplification (Seretan, 2012; Brouwers et al., 2014), and lexical simplification for improving the understanding of medical terms (Grabar et al., 2018)).

While first LS systems (Carroll et al., 1998; Devlin, 1999) used to combine WordNet (Miller, 1998) and frequency information from words, more recent ones are more sophisticated and rely on supervised machine learning methods. Their architecture can be represented with four steps as follows (Shardlow, 2014):

1. Complex Word Identification (CWI): aims to identify target words that need simplification. In CWI, the methods based on large corpora and thesaurus dominate the top 10 in SemEval 2016 (Paetzold and Specia, 2016). In most recent CWI shared task took place in June 2018, word length and word frequency based features lead to the best results.

2. Substitution Generation (SG), to provide candidate substitution for each complex identified word. In SG, Horn et al. (2014) obtain candidates from a parallel corpus contains Wikipedia and simplified version of Wikipedia yielding major step against earlier approaches (Devlin, 1999). Glavaš and Štajner (2015) use word embeddings models to generate candidate substitution leading to even better results.

3. Substitution Selection (SS), to filter out context candidates. Generally, SS first requires all the disambiguation of the candidates provided by the previous step. Only candidates matching the Part-Of-Speech (POS) of the target complex word are retained.

4. Substitute ranking (SR), to sort the retained

[3] `https://cental.uclouvain.be/resyf/`

candidates according to their complexity. In SR, the performance of the state of the art is achieved by the supervised methods: SVM-Rank (Horn et al., 2014) and Boundary Ranking (Paetzold and Specia, 2016). Supervised methods have the caveat of requiring annotated data, nonetheless as consequence they can be adapted according to the target audience.

In practice, this process is not literally respected in LS methods. For some approaches (Biran et al., 2011; Bott et al., 2012; Glavaš and Štajner, 2015), all words are potentially complex and need simplification. Each word is replaced only if it has a simpler synonym. Some other methods merge the SS into the SR step.

Here, we consider the Glavaš and Štajner (2015) method as a baseline of the state of the art. This method is based on the exploitation of general resources in a general context. The baseline relies on word embeddings to generate substitute candidates. Glavaš and Štajner (2015) only replace a target word if it has a lower frequency than the selected candidate substitution. However, we propose a LS method that exploits a new lexical resource, ReSyf (cf. subsection 3.2) which aims to provide simpler substitutes to identified complex words in French, the overall idea being to adapt texts for children who have difficulties with basic reading and comprehension skills in early grades, and who have French as a mother tongue.

3 Lexical Simplification: our method

We present here our methodology to build the LS system. Figure 1 illustrates the architecture of the system that we detail in the next subsections. In brief, we start from a sentence in which complex words have been identified. We then use ReSyf to get candidates for substitution (section 3.2). If the complex word has several meanings, we use automatic word sense disambiguation to select the best set of candidates (section 3.3). The last step consists in selecting the simplest candidate to be used in the simplified sentence (section 3.4).

3.1 Complex Word Identification (CWI)

In this work, we focus our interest on the generation of candidate substitutes in order to improve the quality of the simplification. We use a list of complex reference words that have beforehand been identified as complex by human experts. For example, in the sentence *Le castor est un excellent nageur*[4], the word *excellent* has been tagged as complex.

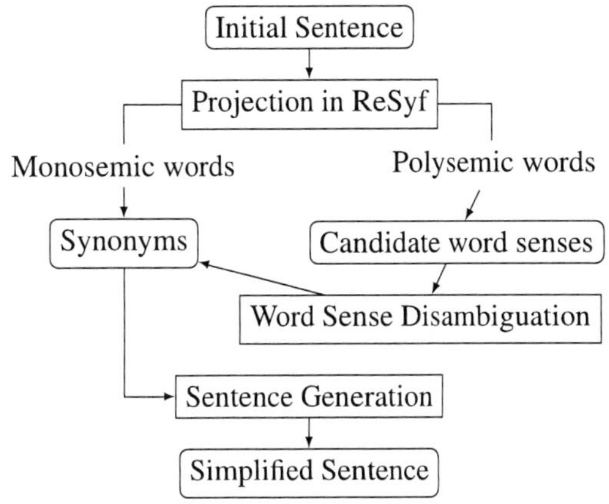

Figure 1: Architecture of the LS system

3.2 Using ReSyf for Lexical Simplification (LS)

ReSyf[5] (Billami et al., 2018) is a lexical resource which includes a disambiguated set of synonyms that are ranked by difficulty. The ranking (order of appearance and weight in the vector) is calculated taking into account intra-lexical features (i.e length of words, syllabic structure, morphological structure, number of orthographical neighbours, etc.), morpho-semantic features (i.e. number of morphemes, frequence of morphemes, polysemy, etc.) and psycholinguistic features (i.e. frequency index, etc.) (François et al., 2016). ReSyf contains more than 57 000 disambiguated lemmas initially extracted from JeuxDeMots[6], a freely available lexical network containing fine-grained semantic information (Lafourcade, 2007).

In order to obtain our synonyms, for each input sentence, complex words are projected in ReSyf. The candidate substitutes are provided by JeuxDeMots and are classified according to the meanings of the complex words. For instance, table 1 shows the candidate substitutes of *excellent* that can be found in ReSyf.

For monosemic words, a list of candidate substitutes, ranked according to their complexity, is directly obtained from ReSyf. For polysemic words like *excellent*, a further disambiguation step

[4] *The beaver is an excellent swimmer.*
[5] `https://cental.uclouvain.be/resyf/`
[6] `http://www.jeuxdemots.org`

Sense	Substitutes
Excellent (délicieux)	*fin, fameux*
Excellent (formidable)	*bon, fort*

Table 1: Senses and substitutes in ReSyf for 'excellent (delicious)' ('fine, well') and 'excellent (great)' ('good, strong')

is applied to choose the most appropriate meaning matching the context of the sentence. ReSyf integrates the generation of candidate substitutes as well as their ranking according to the complexity measure by Billami et al. (2018).

3.3 Word Sense Disambiguation (WSD)

The simplification of *excellent* requires a disambiguation in order to choose a sense among *délicieux* and *formidable* (cf. table 1). To this aim, we apply an algorithm that uses semantic representations for words and word senses (called *semantic signatures*). These signatures have been created and validated by Billami and Gala (2017) and use the structural properties of JeuxDeMots. Furthermore, the ReSyf senses are the same as the senses from JeuxDeMots, encoded with the *semantic refinement* relation.

The semantic signatures that we have used integrate different relationships. Some of these relationships correspond to lexical functions related to the vocabulary itself (such as *associated idea* and *synonymy*) or to hierarchical semantic relations (such as *hypernymy* and *hyponymy*). The algorithm that we propose for complex word sense disambiguation is described below.

First, we initialize the score of each candidate word sense (lines $1-2$). Second, we compare each candidate word sense with each word belonging to the context of the complex word to disambiguate by using semantic signatures (lines $3-5$). Third, for this comparison of each pair (sense, word), we use among others another associative relation defined in JeuxDeMots, named *inhibition*. This relation allows to return, for a given target, the terms that tend to be excluded by this target (line 6). For example, the sense 'excellent (great)' excludes the words *delicious* and *tasty*. The score of the semantic similarity between a candidate word sense and a context word is computed only and only if there is no inhibition relation between them. This way of proceeding to the selection of the words of the context gives the advantage to the senses which

Algorithm 1: Disambiguate a target word by using semantic signatures of words and word senses

Input:
t_w: target word to treat
$sem\_ref\ (t_w)$: senses set for t_w
$CXT(t_w)$: words of the context of t_w, except this latter
Result:
$\hat{\mathbf{Sense}}_{\mathbf{t_w}}$: sense of t_w with the highest score
Data:
$Rels_{Inhib}$: set of pairs of terms whose elements of each pair are linked by the *inhibition relation* with a nonzero positive weight
$S(t)$: a signature for a given term t

1 **Initialization:**
2 $Score_{refs\_C} = \emptyset$ /* associate each sense of t_w with its score. */
3 **for** $sense_i \in sem\_ref(t_w)$ **do**
4 $\quad Score(sense_i) = 0;$
5 $\quad$ **for** $word_j \in CXT(t_w)$, *with* $j \in \{1, \ldots, |CXT(t_w)|\}$ **do**
6 $\quad\quad$ **if** $(sense_i, word_j) \notin Rels_{Inhib}$ **then**
7 $\quad\quad\quad Score(sense_i) = Score(sense_i) + Sim(S(sens_i), S(word_j));$
8 $\quad Score_{refs\_C} \leftarrow Score_{refs\_C} \bigcup (sense_i, Score(sense_i));$
9 **if** $(|$**Best** $(Score_{refs\_C})| \geqslant 2)$ **then**
10 $\quad \hat{\mathbf{Sense}}_{\mathbf{t_w}} \leftarrow$ FIRST$_S(t_w,$ **Best** $(Score_{refs\_C}))$
11 **else**
12 $\quad \hat{\mathbf{Sense}}_{\mathbf{t_w}} \leftarrow$ **Best** $(Score_{refs\_C})$

exclude less words to have a more important score.

The semantic similarity (*i.e.* Sim in algorithm 1) that we use takes into account the relation between two lexical units to compare (Billami and Gala, 2017). If the relation exists between the two elements to compare, we have a perfect similarity else the cosine similarity is estimated by using their semantic signatures (line 7). Fourth, we calculate the score of similarity for each candidate word sense (line 8).

Besides, if there are at least two senses with the highest score, the sense returned by the algorithm is the one with the highest weight in ReSyf (*i.e.* FIRST$_S$ in algorithm 1, lines $9-10$). Otherwise, the one and only best sense is returned (lines 11 – 12). In the previous example, the retained sense for *excellent* is *formidable*.

3.4 Sentence Generation

Once the complex word is disambiguated, the first three ranked synonyms in ReSyf, corresponding to that word-sense, are retained to generate simplified versions of the initial sentence. For instance, the previous sentence can be simplified *Le castor est un bon nageur*[7].

4 Evaluation

Our aim is to assess the use of lexical resource such as ReSyf for the task of lexical simplification. We hypothesise that having already a disambiguated set of synonyms reduces the amount of noisy candidates created by statistical algorithms. To check this hypothesis, we have evaluated the quality of the substitutions produced by the two methods: the baseline based on Glavaš and Štajner (2015) and our method based on ReSyf, relying on the evaluation made by two experts.

4.1 Corpus of Evaluation

The corpus used for evaluation contains literary and scientific texts usually read in classrooms at primary levels (children aged 7 to 9 years old) in France. Within the 187 sentences of the corpus, experts have identified 190 complex words that have to be simplified (thus, we have an average of 1 complex word per sentence).

4.2 Word Embedding for SG

The generation of candidate for substitution by the baseline is based on a Word Embedding model[8] (Fauconnier, 2015) trained on the FrWaC corpus, a "1.6 billion word corpus constructed from the Web limiting the crawl to the .fr domain"[9] and using medium-frequency words as seeds. The corpus was POS-tagged and lemmatized with the TreeTagger[10].

4.3 Human evaluation

In this paper, the simplifications have been evaluated according to their complexity and the context where they appear. Three substitutes are proposed for every complex word. The provided simplifications were assessed by two evaluators following these instructions:

- The substitute must be simpler than the complex word
- The substitute must fit the context of the sentence
- If the complex word appears as a substitute, it is invalidated

The table 2 shows examples of the evaluation. *Beau* and *fort* do not match the context. We computed the inter-rater reliability of the human annotation. Even though selecting good candidates for simplification has been regarded as a complex task for human, we obtained a κ of 0.625 for the baseline model and a κ of 0.656 for the annotation of ReSyf's results.

Based on this human annotation, we have computed two evaluation metrics. *Precision1* is a global precision. Every simplification is considered as an independent sentence. This measure aims to calculate the number of valid simplifications among all the provided ones (*i.e* simplified sentences). *Precision2* allows us to verify, for an initial sentence if, at least, one valid simplification appears among the three proposed ones. For each original sentence, only one valid simplification is counted, even if there are two or three valid ones. If none of the three simplifications are correct, then the count is 0. This measure counts the number of initial sentences that have at least one valid simplification.

$$Precision1 = \frac{\#valid\_simp}{\#all\_simplifications}$$

$$Precision2 = \frac{\#at\_least\_one\_valid\_simp}{\#all\_initial\_sentences}$$

By analysing the simplifications produced by the baseline and our method, table 3 shows that ReSyf provides better results than Word2Vec techniques. In table 3, Precision1 and Precision2 count valid simplifications only if both of the annotators agree on the proposed substitute. This table also shows that our method produces more suitable simplifications (16.3% and 51.9%) than the baseline (15.7% and 49.4%).

[7] *The beaver is a good swimmer.*

[8] http://fauconnier.github.io/#data

[9] http://wacky.sslmit.unibo.it/doku.php?id=corpora

[10] www.cis.uni-muenchen.de/~schmid/tools/TreeTagger

Initial Sentence	Simplified Sentence	Evaluation
Le castor est un **excellent** nageur	Le castor est un **beau** nageur	0
Le castor est un **excellent** nageur	Le castor est un **fort** nageur	0
Le castor est un **excellent** nageur	Le castor est un **bon** nageur	1

Table 2: Evaluation example for simplified versions of the sentence *Le castor est un excellent nageur.*

Methods	**Precision1 (%)**	**Precision2 (%)**
Baseline	15.7	49.4
LS_ReSyf	**16.3**	**51.9**

Table 3: LS evaluation result of annotators 1 and 2

4.4 Discussion

The annotators have noticed that our method provides more linguistically-motivated substitutes than the word2vec method for LS. Indeed, SG from word2vec relies on the distance that separates word vectors. This distance is referred to the context and the general semantic distance that could yield not only appropriate synonyms, but also noise from other less suitable relations like antonymy. However, ReSyf is built from particular semantic relations from JeuxDeMots, especially synonymy and hypernymy which are more suitable for LS. Table 4 shows examples of obtained substitutes from ReSyf and word2vec methods for *marchandise* ('good') and *garçonnet* ('young child').

Complex Word	**Word2Vec Substitute**	**ReSyf Substitute**
Marchandise	transport, douane, commissionnaire	article, produit, marchandise
Garçonnet	fille, père, mère	enfant, garçon, petit

Table 4: Examples of provided substitutes by word2vec and ReSyf methods

Taking into account the difficulty of the task, the evaluation not surprisingly shows that the results are slightly better when the lexical resource ReSyf is used. Word2vec being based on the presence of a lexical unit in a same context, antonyms, wrong hyponyms or wrong senses are to be found among the wrong candidates for lexical substitutions. For instance, the antonym *fin* ('end') is proposed as a substitute for *début* ('beginning') or the sense 'lawyer' is proposed instead of 'bar' for the polysemic French word *barreau*.

Wrong candidates found using ReSyf largely concern cases where multi-word expressions (MWE) are present in the text. As the MWE is currently not detected, we replaced one token of the expression by a simpler synonym that does not necessarily fits the context of the whole expression. For instance, in the expression *se prendre de sympathie* ('sympathize with'), we replaced *sympathie* by simpler candidates such as *interêt* or *accord*. The second candidate clearly does not fit in the global expression, that would ideally need to be substitute as a whole, for example, by *s'occuper de*. ReSyf also proposes "complex words" such as: *long*, *animal* and *présent*. These words are not particularly considered as complex (as regards to their length, frequency or syllable structure). There is currently work in progress to better identify complex words as regards to the difficulties that poor-readers and dyslexic children may have.

5 Conclusion and perspectives

In this paper we have presented a method for lexical substitution that uses a lexical resource where French synonyms are disambiguated and ranked according to the difficulty to be read and understood. The results obtained after the evaluation show that using a lexical resource improves the results (51.9%) as regards to a state-of-the-art system based on word2vec (49.4%). The lexical resource that we have used provides already ranked synonyms, and once the system identifies the complex word to replace, our method is able to provide better candidates for the simplifications.

In future work, we plan (1) to evaluate our method with a greater amount of data and (2) to extend our work to automatically identify complex words in context (CWI). Our final aim is to propose a whole methodology for a lexical simplification system that will adapt texts for French scholars facing difficulties learning to read.

Acknowledgments

This work has been funded by the French Agence Nationale pour la Recherche, through the ALECTOR project (ANR-16-CE28-0005).

References

Sandra Maria Aluísio and Caroline Gasperin. 2010. Fostering digital inclusion and accessibility: the porsimples project for simplification of portuguese texts. In *Proceedings of the NAACL HLT 2010 Young Investigators Workshop on Computational Approaches to Languages of the Americas*, pages 46–53. Association for Computational Linguistics.

Sandra Maria Aluísio, Lucia Specia, Caroline Gasperin, and Carolina Scarton. 2010. Readability assessment for text simplification. In *Proceedings of the NAACL HLT 2010 Fifth Workshop on Innovative Use of NLP for Building Educational Applications*, pages 1–9. Association for Computational Linguistics.

Mokhtar B. Billami, Thomas François, and Núria Gala. 2018. Resyf: a French lexicon with ranked synonyms. In *Proceedings of the 27th International Conference on Computational Linguistics (COLING 2018)*, pages 2570–2581.

Mokhtar B. Billami and Núria Gala. 2017. Creating and validating semantic signatures : application for measuring semantic similarity and lexical substitution. In *The 24th edition of the French NLP conference*, Orleans, France.

Or Biran, Samuel Brody, and Noémie Elhadad. 2011. Putting it simply: a context-aware approach to lexical simplification. In *Proceedings of the 49th Annual Meeting of the Association for Computational Linguistics: Human Language Technologies: short papers-Volume 2*, pages 496–501. Association for Computational Linguistics.

Stefan Bott, Luz Rello, Biljana Drndarevic, and Horacio Saggion. 2012. Can Spanish be simpler? lexsis: Lexical simplification for Spanish. *Proceedings of COLING 2012*, pages 357–374.

Laetitia Brouwers, Delphine Bernhard, Anne-Laure Ligozat, and Thomas François. 2014. Syntactic sentence simplification for French. In *Proceedings of the 3rd Workshop on Predicting and Improving Text Readability for Target Reader Populations (PITR) at EACL 2014*, page 47–56.

John Carroll, Guido Minnen, Yvonne Canning, Siobhan Devlin, and John Tait. 1998. Practical simplification of English newspaper text to assist aphasic readers. In *Proceedings of the AAAI-98 Workshop on Integrating Artificial Intelligence and Assistive Technology*, pages 7–10.

Kevyn Collins-Thompson. 2014. Computational assessment of text readability: A survey of current and future research. *International Journal of Applied Linguistics*, 165(2):97–135.

Siobhan Lucy Devlin. 1999. *Simplifying natural language for aphasic readers.* Ph.D. thesis, University of Sunderland.

William H. DuBay. 2004. *The principles of readability.* Impact Information. Available on http://www.nald.ca/library/research/readab/readab.pdf.

Jean-Philippe Fauconnier. 2015. French word embeddings. http://fauconnier.github.io.

Thomas François, Mokhtar B. Billami, Núria Gala, and Delphine Bernhard. 2016. Bleu, contusion, ecchymose : tri automatique de synonymes en fonction de leur difficulté. In *Actes de la conférence Traitement Automatique des Langues Naturelles*, pages 15–28.

Thomas François and Cédrick Fairon. 2012. An "AI readability" formula for french as a foreign language. In *Proceedings of the 2012 Joint Conference on Empirical Methods in Natural Language Processing and Computational Natural Language Learning*, page 466–477.

Núria Gala and Johannes Ziegler. 2016. Reducing lexical complexity as a tool to increase text accessibility for children with dyslexia. In *Proceedings of the Workshop on Computational Linguistics for Linguistic Complexity (CL4LC), COLING 2014*, pages 59–66.

Goran Glavaš and Sanja Štajner. 2015. Simplifying lexical simplification: do we need simplified corpora? In *Proceedings of the 53rd Annual Meeting of the Association for Computational Linguistics and the 7th International Joint Conference on Natural Language Processing (Volume 2: Short Papers)*, volume 2, pages 63–68.

Natalia Grabar, Emmanuel Farce, and Laurent Sparrow. 2018. Étude de la lisibilité des documents de santé avec des méthodes d'oculométrie. In *Proceedings of the Conference Traitement Automatique des Langues Naturelles.*

Colby Horn, Cathryn Manduca, and David Kauchak. 2014. Learning a lexical simplifier using wikipedia. In *Proceedings of the 52nd Annual Meeting of the Association for Computational Linguistics (Volume 2: Short Papers)*, volume 2, pages 458–463.

Robin Keskisärkkä. 2012. Automatic text simplification via synonym replacement. Master's thesis, Dept of Computer and Information Science at Linkoping University, Sweden.

Mathieu Lafourcade. 2007. Making people play for lexical acquisition. In *In Proc. SNLP 2007, 7th Symposium on Natural Language Processing*.

Aurélien Max. 2006. Writing for language-impaired readers. In *Proc. of Computational Linguistics and Intelligent Text Processing: 7th International Conference, CICLing 2006*, page 567–570, Mexico City, Mexico.

George Miller. 1998. *WordNet: An electronic lexical database*. MIT press.

Gustavo Paetzold and Lucia Specia. 2016. Semeval 2016 task 11: Complex word identification. In *Proceedings of the 10th International Workshop on Semantic Evaluation (SemEval-2016)*, pages 560–569.

Gustavo Paetzold and Lucia Specia. 2017. A survey on lexical simplification. *Journal of Artificial Intelligence Research*, 60:549–593.

Luz Rello, Ricardo Baeza-Yates, Stefan Bott, and Horacio Saggion. 2013a. Simplify or help?: Text simplification strategies for people with dyslexia. In *Proceedings of the 10th International Cross-Disciplinary Conference on Web Accessibility*, page 15. ACM.

Luz Rello, Ricardo Baeza-Yates, Laura Dempere-Marco, and Horacio Saggion. 2013b. Frequent words improve readability and short words improve understandability for people with dyslexia. In *IFIP Conference on Human-Computer Interaction*, pages 203–219. Springer.

Luz Rello, Clara Bayarri, Azuki Górriz, Ricardo Baeza-Yates, Saurabh Gupta, Gaurang Kanvinde, Horacio Saggion, Stefan Bott, Roberto Carlini, and Vasile Topac. 2013c. Dyswebxia 2.0!: more accessible text for people with dyslexia. In *Proceedings of the 10th International Cross-Disciplinary Conference on Web Accessibility*, page 25. ACM.

Horacio Saggion. 2017. Automatic text simplification. *Synthesis Lectures on Human Language Technologies*, 10(1):1–137.

V. Seretan. 2012. Acquisition of syntactic simplification rules for french. In *Proceedings of the eight international conference on language resources and evaluation (LREC'12)*, pages 4019–4026.

Matthew Shardlow. 2014. A survey of automated text simplification. *International Journal of Advanced Computer Science and Applications*, 4(1):58–70.

Donatella Spinelli, Maria De Luca, Gloria Di Filippo, Monica Mancini, Marialuisa Martelli, and Pierluigi Zoccolotti. 2005. Length effect in word naming in reading: Role of reading experience and reading deficit in italian readers. *Developmental neuropsychology*, 27(2):217–235.

Johannes C. Ziegler, Conrad Perry, Anna Ma-Wyatt, Diana Ladner, and Gerd Schulte-Körne. 2003. Developmental dyslexia in different languages: Language-specific or universal? *Journal of experimental child psychology*, 86(3):169–193.

Reference-less Quality Estimation of Text Simplification Systems

Louis Martin
Facebook AI Research & Inria
louismartin@fb.com

Samuel Humeau
Facebook AI Research
samuelhumeau@fb.com

Pierre-Emmanuel Mazaré
Facebook AI Research
pem@fb.com

Antoine Bordes
Facebook AI Research
abordes@fb.com

Éric de La Clergerie
Inria
eric.de_la_clergerie@inria.fr

Benoît Sagot
Inria
benoit.sagot@inria.fr

Abstract

The evaluation of text simplification (TS) systems remains an open challenge. As the task has common points with machine translation (MT), TS is often evaluated using MT metrics such as BLEU. However, such metrics require high quality reference data, which is rarely available for TS. TS has the advantage over MT of being a monolingual task, which allows for direct comparisons to be made between the simplified text and its original version. In this paper, we compare multiple approaches to reference-less quality estimation of sentence-level text simplification systems, based on the dataset used for the QATS 2016 shared task. We distinguish three different dimensions: grammaticality, meaning preservation and simplicity. We show that n-gram-based MT metrics such as BLEU and METEOR correlate the most with human judgment of grammaticality and meaning preservation, whereas simplicity is best evaluated by basic length-based metrics.

1 Introduction

Text simplification (hereafter TS) has received increasing interest by the scientific community in recent years. It aims at producing a simpler version of a source text that is both easier to read and to understand, thus improving the accessibility of text for people suffering from a range of disabilities such as aphasia (Carroll et al., 1998) or dyslexia (Rello et al., 2013), as well as for second language learners (Xia et al., 2016) and people with low literacy (Watanabe et al., 2009). This topic has been researched for a variety of languages such as English (Zhu et al., 2010; Wubben et al., 2012; Narayan and Gardent, 2014; Xu et al., 2015), French (Brouwers et al., 2014), Spanish (Saggion et al., 2011), Portuguese (Specia, 2010), Italian (Brunato et al., 2015) and Japanese (Goto et al., 2015).[1]

One of the main challenges in TS is finding an adequate automatic evaluation metric, which is necessary to avoid the time-consuming human evaluation. Any TS evaluation metric should take into account three properties expected from the output of a TS system, namely:

- Grammaticality: how grammatically correct is the TS system output?
- Meaning preservation: how well is the meaning of the source sentence preserved in the TS system output?
- Simplicity: how simple is the TS system output?[2]

TS is often reduced to a sentence-level problem, whereby one sentence is transformed into a simpler version containing one or more sentences. In this paper, we shall make use of the terms *source (sentence)* and *(TS system) output* to respectively denote a sentence given as an input to a TS system and the simplified, single or multi-sentence output produced by the system.

TS, seen as a sentence-level problem, is often viewed as a monolingual variant of (sentence-level) MT. The standard approach to automatic TS evaluation is therefore to view the task as a translation problem and to use machine translation (MT)

[1] Note that text simplification has also been used as a preprocessing step for other natural language processing tasks such as machine translation (Chandrasekar et al., 1996) and semantic role labelling (Vickrey and Koller, 2008).

[2] There is no unique way to define the notion of *simplicity* in this context. Previous works often rely on the intuition of human annotators to evaluate the level of simplicity of a TS system output.

Proceedings of the 1st Workshop on Automatic Text Adaptation (ATA), pages 29–38,
Tilburg, The Netherlands, November 8 2018.

evaluation metrics such as BLEU (Papineni et al., 2002). However, MT evaluation metrics rely on the existence of parallel corpora of source sentences and manually produced reference translations, which are available on a large scale for many language pairs (Tiedemann, 2012). TS datasets are less numerous and smaller. Moreover, they are often automatically extracted from comparable corpora rather than strictly parallel corpora, which results in noisier reference data. For example, the PWKP dataset (Zhu et al., 2010) consists of 100,000 sentences from the English Wikipedia automatically aligned with sentences from the Simple English Wikipedia based on term-based similarity metrics. It has been shown by Xu et al. (2015) that many of PWKP's "simplified" sentences are in fact not simpler or even not related to their corresponding source sentence. Even if better quality corpora such as Newsela do exist (Xu et al., 2015), they are costly to create, often of limited size, and not necessarily open-access.

This creates a challenge for the use of reference-based MT metrics for TS evaluation. However, TS has the advantage of being a monolingual translation-like task, the source being in the same language as the output. This allows for new, non-conventional ways to use MT evaluation metrics, namely by using them to compare the output of a TS system with the source sentence, thus avoiding the need for reference data. However, such an evaluation method can only capture at most two of the three above-mentioned dimensions, namely meaning preservation and, to a lesser extent, grammaticality.

Previous works on reference-less TS evaluation include Štajner et al. (2014), who compare the behaviour of six different MT metrics when used between the source sentence and the corresponding simplified output. They evaluate these metrics with respect to meaning preservation and grammaticality. We extend their work in two directions. Firstly, we extend the comparison to include the degree of simplicity achieved by the system. Secondly, we compare additional features, including those used by Štajner et al. (2016a), both individually, as elementary metrics, and within multi-feature metrics. To our knowledge, no previous work has provided as thorough a comparison across such a wide range and combination of features for the reference-less evaluation of TS.

First we review available text simplification evaluation methods and traditional quality estimation features. We then present the QATS shared task and the associated dataset, which we use for our experiments. Finally we compare all methods in a reference-less setting and analyze the results.

2 Existing evaluation methods

2.1 Using MT metrics to compare the output and a reference

TS can be considered as a monolingual translation task. As a result, MT metrics such as BLEU (Papineni et al., 2002), which compare the output of an MT system to a reference translation, have been extensively used for TS (Narayan and Gardent, 2014; Štajner et al., 2015; Xu et al., 2016). Other successful MT metrics include TER (Snover et al., 2009), ROUGE (Lin, 2004) and METEOR (Banerjee and Lavie, 2005), but they have not gained much traction in the TS literature.

These metrics rely on good quality references, something which is often not available in TS, as discussed by Xu et al. (2015). Moreover, Štajner et al. (2015) and Sulem et al. (2018a) showed that using BLEU to compare the system output with a reference is not a good way to perform TS evaluation, even when good quality references are available. This is especially true when the TS system produces more than one sentence for a single source sentence.

2.2 Using MT metrics to compare the output and the source sentence

As mentioned in the Introduction, the fact that TS is a monolingual task means that MT metrics can also be used to compare a system output with its corresponding source sentence, thus avoiding the need for reference data. Following this idea, Štajner et al. (2014) found encouraging correlations between 6 widely used MT metrics and human assessments of grammaticality and meaning preservation. However MT metrics are not relevant for the evaluation of simplicity, which is why they did not take this dimension into account. Xu et al. (2016) also explored the idea of comparing the TS system output with its corresponding source sentence, but their metric, SARI, also requires to compare the output with a reference. In fact, this metric is designed to take advantage of more than one reference. It can be applied when only one reference is available for each source sentence, but its results are better when multiple references are available.

Attempts to perform Quality Estimation on the output of TS systems, without using references, include the 2016 Quality Assessment for Text Simplification (QATS) shared task (Štajner et al., 2016b), to which we shall come back in section 3. Sulem et al. (2018b) introduce another approach, named SAMSA. The idea is to evaluate the structural simplicity of a TS system output given the corresponding source sentence. SAMSA is maximized when the simplified text is a sequence of short and simple sentences, each accounting for one semantic event in the original sentence. It relies on an in-depth analysis of the source sentence and the corresponding output, based on a semantic parser and a word aligner. A drawback of this approach is that good quality semantic parsers are only available for a handful of languages. The intuition that sentence splitting is an important sub-task for producing simplified text motivated Narayan et al. (2017) to organize the *Split and Rephrase* shared task, which was dedicated to this problem.

2.3 Other metrics

One can also estimate the quality of a TS system output based on simple features extracted from it.

For instance, the QUEST framework for quality estimation in MT gives a number of useful baseline features for evaluating an output sentence (Specia et al., 2013). These features range from simple statistics, such as the number of words in the sentence, to more sophisticated features, such as the probability of the sentence according to a language model. Several teams who participated in the QATS shared task used metrics based on this framework, namely SMH (Štajner et al., 2016a), UoLGP (Rios and Sharoff, 2015) and UoW (Béchara et al., 2015).

Readability metrics such as Flesch-Kincaid Grade Level (FKGL) and Flesch Reading Ease (FRE) (Kincaid et al., 1975) have been extensively used for evaluating simplicity. These two metrics, which were shown experimentally to give good results, are linear combinations of the number of words per sentence and the number of syllables per word, using carefully adjusted weights.

3 Methodology

Our goal is to compare a large number of ways to perform TS evaluation without a reference. To

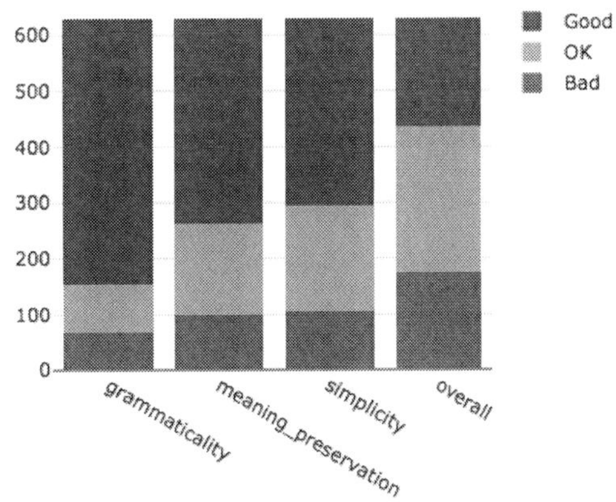

Figure 1: Label repartition on the QATS Shared task

this end, we use the dataset provided in the QATS shared task. We first compare the behaviour of elementary metrics, which range from commonly used metrics such as BLEU to basic metrics based on a single low-level feature such as sentence length. We then compare the effect of aggregating these elementary metrics into more complex ones and compare our results with the state of the art, based on the QATS shared task data and results.

3.1 The QATS shared task

The data from the QATS shared task (Štajner et al., 2016b) consists of a collection of 631 pairs of english sentences composed of a source sentence extracted from an online corpus and a simplified version thereof, which can contain one or more sentences. This collection is split into a training set (505 sentence pairs) and a test set (126 sentence pairs). Simplified versions were produced automatically using one of several TS systems trained by the shared task organizers. Human annotators labelled each sentence pair using one of the three labels *Good*, *OK* and *Bad* on each of the three dimensions: grammaticality, meaning preservation and simplicity[3]. An overall quality label was then automatically assigned to each sentence pair based on its three manually assigned labels using a method detailed in (Štajner et al., 2016b). Distribution of the labels and examples are presented in FIGURE 1 and TABLE 1.

The goal of the shared task is, for each sentence in the test set, to either produce a label (*Good*, *OK*,

[3]We were not able to find detailed information about the annotation process. In particular, we do not know whether each sentence was annotated only once or whether multiple annotations were produced, followed by an adjudication step.

Version	Sentence	G	M	S	O	Modification
		Aspect				
Original	All three were arrested in the Toome area **and** have been taken to the Serious Crime Suite at Antrim police station.	good	good	good	good	syntactic
Simple	All three were arrested in the Toome area. **All three** have been taken to the Serious Crime Suite at Antrim police station.					
Original	For years the former Bosnia Serb army commander Ratko Mladic had evaded capture **and was one of the worlds most wanted men, but his time on the run finally ended last year when he was arrested near Belgrade.**	good	bad	ok	bad	content reduction
Simple	For years the former Bosnia Serb army commander Ratko Mladic had evaded capture.					
Original	Madrid was occupied by French troops during the Napoleonic Wars, and Napoleons brother Joseph was **installed** on the throne.	good	good	good	good	lexical
Simple	Madrid was occupied by French troops during the Napoleonic Wars, and Napoleons brother Joseph was **put** on the throne.					
Original	Keeping articles with potential **encourages** editors, especially unregistered users, to be bold and improve the article to allow it to evolve over time.	bad	bad	ok	bad	dropping
Simple	Keeping articles with potential editors, especially unregistered users, to be bold and improve the article to allow it to evolve over time.					

Table 1: Examples from the training dataset of QATS. Differences between the original and the simplified version are presented in bold. This table is adapted from Štajner et al. (2016b).

Bad) or a raw score estimating the overall quality of the simplification for each of the three dimensions. Raw score predictions are evaluated using the Pearson correlation with the ground truth labels, while actual label prediction are evaluated using the weighted F1-score. The shared task is described in further details on the QATS website[4].

3.2 Features

In our experiments, we compared about 60 elementary metrics, which can be organised as follows:

- MT metrics
  - BLEU, ROUGE, METEOR, TERp
  - Variants of BLEU: BLEU_1gram, BLEU_2gram, BLEU_3gram, BLEU_4gram and seven smoothing methods[5] from NLTK (Bird and Loper, 2004).
  - Intermediate components of TERp inspired by (Štajner et al., 2016a): e.g. number of insertions, deletions, shifts...
- Readability metrics and other sentence-level features: FKGL and FRE, numbers of words, characters, syllables...
- Metrics based on the baseline QuEst features (17 features) (Specia et al., 2013), such as statistics on the number of words, word lengths, language model probability and n-gram frequency.
- Metrics based on other features: frequency table position, concreteness as extracted from Brysbaert et al.'s 2014 list, language model probability of words using a convolutional sequence to sequence model from (Gehring et al., 2017), comparison methods using pre-trained fastText word embeddings (Mikolov et al., 2018) or Skip-thought sentence embeddings (Kiros et al., 2015).

TABLE 2 lists 30 of the elementary metrics that we compared, which are those that we found to correlate the most with human judgments on one or more of the three dimensions (grammaticality, meaning preservation, simplicity).

3.3 Experimental setup

Evaluation of elementary metrics We rank all features by comparing their behaviour with human

[4] http://qats2016.github.io/shared.html

[5] https://www.nltk.org/api/nltk.translate.html#nltk.translate.bleu_score.SmoothingFunction

judgments on the training set. We first compute for each elementary metric the Pearson correlation between its results and the manually assigned labels for each of the three dimensions. We then rank our elementary metrics according to the absolute value of the Pearson correlation.[6]

Training and evaluation of a combined metric We use our elementary metrics as features to train classifiers on the training set, and evaluate their performance on the test set. We therefore scale them and reduce the dimensionality with a 25-component PCA[7], then train several regression algorithms[8] and classification algorithms[9] using scikit-learn (Pedregosa et al., 2011). For each dimension, we keep the two models performing best on the test set and add them in the leaderboard of the QATS shared task (TABLE 4), naming them with the name of the regression algorithm they were built with.

4 Results

4.1 Comparing elementary metrics

FIGURE 3 ranks all elementary metrics given their absolute Pearson correlation on each of the three dimensions.

Grammaticality N-gram based MT metrics have the highest correlation with human grammaticality judgments. METEOR seems to be the best, probably because of its robustness to synonymy, followed by smoothed BLEU (BLEUSmoothed in 2). This indicates that relevant grammaticality information can be derived from the source sentence. We were expecting that information contained in a language model would help achieving better results (*AvgLMProbsOutput*), but MT metrics correlate better with human judgments. We deduce that the grammaticality information contained in the source is more specific and more helpful for evaluation than what is learned by the language model.

[6]We will release our code on github.

[7]We used PCA instead of feature selection because it performed better on the validation set. The number of component was tuned on the validation set as well.

[8]Regressors: Linear regression, Lasso, Ridge, Linear SVR (SVM regressor), Adaboost regressor, Gradient boosting regressor and Random forest regressor.

[9]Classifiers: Logistic regression, MLP classifier (with L2 penalty, alpha=1), SVC (linear SVM classifier), K-nearsest neighbors classifier (k=3), Adaboost classifier, Gradient boosting classifier and Random forest classifier.

Meaning preservation It is not surprising that meaning preservation is best evaluated using MT metrics that compare the source sentence to the output sentence, with in particular smoothed BLEU, BLEU_3gram and METEOR. Very simple features such as the percentage of words in common between source and output also rank high. Surprisingly, word embedding comparison methods do not perform as well for meaning preservation, even when using word alignment.

Simplicity Methods that give the best results are the most straightforward for assessing simplicity, namely word, character and syllable counts in the output, averaged over the number of output sentences. These simple features even outperform the traditional, more complex metrics FKGL and FRE. As could be expected, we find that metrics with the highest correlation to human simplicity judgments only take the output into account. Exceptions are the *NBSourceWords* and *NBSourcePunct* features. Indeed, if the source sentence has a lot of words and punctuation, and is therefore likely to be particularly complex, then the output will most likely be less simple as well. We also expected word concreteness ratings and position in the frequency table to be good indicators of simplicity, but it does not seem to be the case here. Structural simplicity might simply be more important than such more sophisticated components of the human intuition of simple text.

Discussion Even if counting the number of words or comparing n-grams are good proxies for the simplification quality, they are still very superficial features and might miss some deeper and more complex information. Moreover the fact that grammaticality and meaning preservation are best evaluated using n-gram-based comparison metrics might bias the TS models towards copying the source sentence and applying fewer modifications.

Syntactic parsing or language modelling might capture more insightful grammatical information and allow for more flexibility in the simplification model. Regarding meaning preservation, semantic analysis or paraphrase detection models would also be good candidates for a deeper analysis.

Warning note We should be careful when interpreting these results as the QATS dataset is relatively small. We compute confidence intervals on our results, and find them to be non-negligible, yet without putting our general observations into

Short name	Description
NBSourcePunct	Number of punctuation tokens in source (QuEst)
NBSourceWords	Number of source words (QuEst)
NBOutputPunct	Number of punctuation tokens in output (QuEst)
TypeTokenRatio	Type token ratio (QuEst)
TERp_Del	Number of deletions (TERp component)
TERp_NumEr	Number of total errors (TERp component)
TERp_Sub	Number of substitutions (TERp component)
TERp	TERp MT metric
BLEU_1gram	BLEU MT metric with unigrams only
BLEU_2gram	BLEU MT metric up to bigrams
BLEU_3gram	BLEU MT metric up to trigrams
BLEU_4gram	BLEU MT metric up to 4-grams
METEOR	METEOR MT metric
ROUGE	ROUGE summarization metric
BLEUSmoothed	BLEU MT metric with smoothing (method 7 from nltk)
AvgCosineSim	Cosine similarity between source and output pre-trained word embeddings
NBOutputChars	Number of characters in the output
NBOutputCharsPerSent	Average number of characters per sentence in the output
NBOutputSyllables	Number of syllables in the output
NBOutputSyllablesPerSent	Average number of syllables per sentence in the output
NBOutputWords	Number of words in the output
NBOutputWordsPerSent	Average number of words per sentence in the output
AvgLMProbsOutput	Average log-probabilities of output words (Language Model)
MinLMProbsOutput	Minimum log-probability of output words (Language Model)
MaxPosInFreqTable	Maximum position of output words in the frequency table
AvgConcreteness	Average word concreteness Brysbaert et al.'s 2014 concreteness list
OutputFKGL	Flesch-Kincaid Grade Level
OutputFRE	Flesch Reading Ease
WordsInCommon	Percentage of words in common between source and Output

Table 2: Brief description of 30 of our most relevant elementary metrics

Grammaticality			Meaning Preservation			Simplicity		
Short name	Train ↓	Test	Short name	Train ↓	Test	Short name	Train ↓	Test
Best QATS team		0.48	*Best QATS team*		0.59	*Best QATS team*		0.38
METEOR	0.36	0.39	BLEUSmoothed	0.59	0.52	NBOutputCharsPerSent	-0.52	-0.45
BLEUSmoothed	0.33	0.34	BLEU_3gram	0.57	0.52	NBOutputSyllablesPerSent	-0.52	-0.49
BLEU_4gram	0.32	0.34	METEOR	0.57	0.58	NBOutputWordsPerSent	-0.51	-0.39
BLEU_3gram	0.31	0.34	BLEU_2gram	0.57	0.52	NBOutputChars	-0.48	-0.37
TERp_NumEr	-0.30	-0.31	BLEU_4gram	0.57	0.51	NBOutputWords	-0.47	-0.29
BLEU_2gram	0.30	0.34	WordsInCommon	0.55	0.50	NBOutputSyllables	-0.46	-0.42
TERp	-0.30	-0.32	BLEU_1gram	0.55	0.52	NBOutputPunt	-0.42	-0.31
ROUGE	0.29	0.29	ROUGE	0.55	0.47	NBSourceWords	-0.38	-0.21
AvgLMProbsOutput	0.28	0.34	TERp	-0.54	-0.48	outputFKGL	-0.36	-0.37
BLEU_1gram	0.27	0.33	TERp_NumEr	-0.53	-0.49	NBSourcePunct	-0.34	-0.18
WordsInCommon	0.27	0.30	TERp_Del	-0.50	-0.52	TypeTokenRatio	-0.22	-0.04
TERp_Del	-0.27	-0.35	AvgCosineSim	0.44	0.34	AvgConcreteness	0.21	0.32
NBSourceWords	-0.25	-0.07	AvgLMProbsOutput	0.39	0.36	MaxPosInFreqTable	-0.18	0.03
AvgCosineSim	0.23	0.25	AvgConcreteness	-0.28	-0.06	MinLMProbsOutput	0.17	0.15
MinLMProbsOutput	0.11	-0.07	NBSourceWords	-0.28	-0.13	OutputFRE	0.16	0.27

Table 3: Pearson correlation with human judgments of elementary metrics ranked by absolute value on training set (15 best metrics for each dimension).

question. For instance, METEOR, which performs best on grammaticality, has a 95% confidence interval of 0.36 ± 0.08 on the training set. These results are therefore preliminary and should be validated on other datasets.

4.2 Combination of all features with trained models

We also combine all elementary metrics and train an evaluation models for each of the three dimensions. TABLE 4a presents our two best regressors in validation for each of the dimensions and TABLE 4b for classifiers.

Pearson correlation for regressors (raw scoring) Combining the features does not bring a clear advantage over the elementary metrics METEOR and NBOutputSyllablesPerSent. Indeed our best models score respectively on grammaticality, meaning preservation and simplicity: 0.33 (Lasso), 0.58 (Ridge) and 0.49 (Ridge) versus 0.39 (METEOR), 0.58 (METEOR) and 0.49 (NBOutputSyllablesPerSent).

It is surprising to us that the aggregation of multiple elementary features would score worse than the features themselves. However, we observe a strong discrepancy between the scores obtained on the train and test set, as illustrated by TABLE 3. We also observed very large confidence intervals in terms of Pearson correlation. For instance our lasso model scores 0.33 ± 0.17 on the test set for grammaticality. This should observe caution when interpreting Pearson scores on QATS.

F1-score for classifiers (assigning labels) On the classification task, our models seem to score best for meaning preservation, simplicity and overall, and third for grammaticality. This seems to confirm the importance of considering a large ensemble of elementary features including length-based metrics to evaluate simplicity.

5 Conclusion

Finding accurate ways to evaluate text simplification (TS) without the need for reference data is a key challenge for TS, both for exploring new approaches and for optimizing current models, in particular those relying on unsupervised, often MT-inspired models.

We explore multiple reference-less quality evaluation methods for automatic TS systems, based on data from the 2016 QATS shared task. We rely on the three key dimensions of the quality of a TS system: grammaticality, meaning preservation and simplicity.

Our results show that grammaticality and meaning preservation are best assessed using n-gram-based MT metrics evaluated between the output and the source sentence. In particular, METEOR and smoothed BLEU achieve the highest correlation with human judgments. These approaches even outperform metrics that make an extensive use of external data, such as language models. This shows that a lot of useful information can be obtained from the source sentence itself.

Regarding simplicity, we observe that counting the number of characters, syllables and words provides the best results. In other words, given the currently available metrics, the length of a sentence seems to remain the best available proxy for its simplicity.

However, given the small size of the QATS dataset and the high variance observed in our experiments, these results must be taken with a pinch of salt and will need to be confirmed on a larger dataset. Creating a larger annotated dataset as well as averaging multiple human annotations for each pair of sentences would help reducing the variance of the experiments and confirming our findings.

In future work, we shall explore richer and more complex features extracted using syntactic and semantic analyzers, such as those used by the SAMSA metric, and paraphrase detection models.

Finally, it remains to be understood how we can optimize the trade-off between grammaticality, meaning preservation and simplicity, in order to build the best possible comprehensive TS metric in terms of correlation with human judgments. Unsurprisingly, optimizing one of these dimensions often leads to lower results on other dimensions (Schwarzer and Kauchak, 2018). For instance, the best way to guarantee grammaticality and meaning preservation is to leave the source sentence unchanged, thus resulting in no simplification at all. Improving TS systems will require better global TS evaluation metrics. This is especially true when considering that TS is in fact a multiply defined task, as there are many different ways of simplifying a text, depending on the different categories of people and applications at whom TS is aimed.

Grammaticality	Meaning Preservation	Simplicity	Overall
0.482 OSVCML1	0.588 IIT-Meteor	0.487 **Ridge**	0.423 **Ridge**
0.384 METEOR	0.585 OSVCML	0.456 **LinearSVR**	0.423 **LinearRegression**
0.344 BLEU	0.575 **Ridge**	0.382 OSVCML1	0.343 OSVCML2
0.340 OSVCML	0.573 OSVCML2	0.376 OSVCML2	0.334 OSVCML
0.327 **Lasso**	0.555 **Lasso**	0.339 OSVCML	0.232 SimpleNets-RNN2
0.323 TER	0.533 BLEU	0.320 SimpleNets-MLP	0.230 OSVCML1
0.308 SimpleNets-MLP	0.527 METEOR	0.307 SimpleNets-RNN3	0.205 UoLGP-emb
0.308 WER	0.513 TER	0.240 SimpleNets-RNN2	0.198 SimpleNets-MLP
0.256 UoLGP-emb	0.495 WER	0.123 UoLGP-combo	0.196 METEOR
0.256 UoLGP-combo	0.482 OSVCML1	0.120 UoLGP-emb	0.189 UoLGP-combo
0.208 UoLGP-quest	0.465 SimpleNets-MLP	0.086 UoLGP-quest	0.144 UoLGP-quest
0.118 **GradientBoostingRegressor**	0.285 UoLGP-quest	0.052 IIT-S	0.130 TER
0.064 SimpleNets-RNN3	0.262 SimpleNets-RNN2	-0.169 METEOR	0.112 SimpleNets-RNN3
0.056 SimpleNets-RNN2	0.262 SimpleNets-RNN3	-0.242 TER	0.111 WER
	0.250 UoLGP-combo	-0.260 WER	0.107 BLEU
	0.188 UoLGP-emb	-0.267 BLEU	

(a) Pearson correlation for regressors (raw scoring)

Grammaticality	Meaning Preservation	Simplicity	Overall
71.84 SMH-RandForest	70.14 **SVC**	61.60 **SVC**	49.61 **LogisticRegression**
71.64 SMH-IBk	68.07 SMH-Logistic	56.95 **AdaBoostClassifier**	48.57 SMH-RandForest-b
70.43 **LogisticRegression**	65.60 MS-RandForest	56.42 SMH-RandForest-b	48.20 UoW
69.96 SMH-RandForest-b	64.40 SMH-RandForest	53.02 SMH-RandForest	47.54 SMH-Logistic
69.09 BLEU	63.74 TER	51.12 SMH-IBk	46.06 SimpleNets-RNN2
68.82 SimpleNets-MLP	63.54 SimpleNets-MLP	49.96 SimpleNets-RNN3	45.71 **AdaBoostClassifier**
68.36 TER	62.82 BLEU	49.81 SimpleNets-MLP	44.50 SMH-RandForest
67.60 **GradientBoosting**	62.72 MT-baseline	48.31 MT-baseline	40.94 METEOR
67.53 MS-RandForest	62.69 IIT-Meteor	47.84 MS-IBk-b	40.75 SimpleNets-RNN3
67.50 IIT-LM	61.71 MS-IBk-b	47.82 MS-RandForest	39.85 MS-RandForest
66.79 WER	61.50 MS-IBk	47.47 SimpleNets-RNN2	39.80 DeepIndiBow
66.75 MS-RandForest-b	60.38 **GradientBoosting**	43.46 IIT-S	39.30 IIT-Metrics
65.89 DeepIndiBow	60.12 METEOR	42.57 DeepIndiBow	38.27 MS-IBk
65.89 DeepBow	59.69 SMH-RandForest-b	40.92 UoW	38.16 MS-IBk-b
65.89 MT-baseline	59.06 WER	39.68 Majority-class	38.03 DeepBow
65.89 Majority-class	58.83 UoW	38.10 MS-IBk	37.49 MT-baseline
65.72 METEOR	51.29 SimpleNets-RNN2	35.58 DeepBow	34.08 TER
65.50 SimpleNets-RNN2	51.00 CLaC-RF	34.88 CLaC-RF-0.5	34.06 CLaC-0.5
65.11 SimpleNets-RNN3	46.64 SimpleNets-RNN3	34.66 CLaC-RF-0.6	33.69 SimpleNets-MLP
64.39 CLaC-RF-Perp	46.30 DeepBow	34.48 WER	33.04 IIT-Default
62.00 MS-IBk	42.53 DeepIndiBow	34.30 CLaC-RF-0.7	32.92 BLEU
46.32 UoW	42.51 Majority-class	33.52 TER	32.88 CLaC-0.7
		33.34 METEOR	32.20 CLaC-0.6
		33.00 BLEU	31.28 WER
			26.53 Majority-class

(b) Weighted F1 Score for classifiers (assign the label Good, OK or Bad)

Table 4: QATS leaderboard. Results in **bold** are our additions to the original leaderboard. We only select the two models that rank highest during cross-validation.

Acknowledgments

We would like to thank our anonymous reviewers for their insightful comments.

References

Satanjeev Banerjee and Alon Lavie. 2005. Meteor: An automatic metric for mt evaluation with improved correlation with human judgments. In *Proceedings of the acl workshop on intrinsic and extrinsic evaluation measures for machine translation and/or summarization*, pages 65–72.

Hanna Béchara, Hernani Costa, Shiva Taslimipoor, Rohit Gupta, Constantin Orasan, Gloria Corpas Pastor, and Ruslan Mitkov. 2015. Miniexperts: An svm approach for measuring semantic textual similarity. In *Proceedings of the 9th international workshop on semantic evaluation (SemEval 2015)*, pages 96–101.

Steven Bird and Edward Loper. 2004. Nltk: the natural language toolkit. In *Proceedings of the ACL 2004 on Interactive poster and demonstration sessions*, page 31. Association for Computational Linguistics.

Laetitia Brouwers, Delphine Bernhard, Anne-Laure Ligozat, and Thomas François. 2014. Syntactic sentence simplification for french. In *Proceedings of the 3rd Workshop on Predicting and Improving Text Readability for Target Reader Populations (PITR)*, pages 47–56.

Dominique Brunato, Felice Dell'Orletta, Giulia Venturi, and Simonetta Montemagni. 2015. Design and annotation of the first italian corpus for text simplification. In *Proceedings of The 9th Linguistic Annotation Workshop*, pages 31–41.

Marc Brysbaert, Amy Beth Warriner, and Victor Kuperman. 2014. Concreteness ratings for 40 thousand generally known english word lemmas. *Behavior research methods*, 46(3):904–911.

John Carroll, Guido Minnen, Yvonne Canning, Siobhan Devlin, and John Tait. 1998. Practical simplification of english newspaper text to assist aphasic readers. In *Proceedings of the AAAI-98 Workshop on Integrating Artificial Intelligence and Assistive Technology*, pages 7–10.

Raman Chandrasekar, Christine Doran, and Bangalore Srinivas. 1996. Motivations and methods for text simplification. In *Proceedings of the 16th conference on Computational linguistics-Volume 2*, pages 1041–1044. Association for Computational Linguistics.

Jonas Gehring, Michael Auli, David Grangier, Denis Yarats, and Yann N. Dauphin. 2017. Convolutional sequence to sequence learning. *arXiv preprint arXiv:1705.03122*.

Isao Goto, Hideki Tanaka, and Tadashi Kumano. 2015. Japanese news simplification: Task design, data set construction, and analysis of simplified text. *Proceedings of MT Summit XV*, 1:17–31.

J. Peter Kincaid, Robert P Fishburne Jr., Richard L. Rogers, and Brad S. Chissom. 1975. Derivation of new readability formulas (automated readability index, fog count and flesch reading ease formula) for navy enlisted personnel.

Ryan Kiros, Yukun Zhu, Ruslan R Salakhutdinov, Richard Zemel, Raquel Urtasun, Antonio Torralba, and Sanja Fidler. 2015. Skip-thought vectors. In *Advances in neural information processing systems*, pages 3294–3302.

Chin-Yew Lin. 2004. Rouge: A package for automatic evaluation of summaries. *Text Summarization Branches Out*.

Tomas Mikolov, Edouard Grave, Piotr Bojanowski, Christian Puhrsch, and Armand Joulin. 2018. Advances in pre-training distributed word representations. In *Proceedings of the International Conference on Language Resources and Evaluation (LREC 2018)*.

Shashi Narayan and Claire Gardent. 2014. Hybrid simplification using deep semantics and machine translation. In *Proceedings of the 52nd Annual Meeting of the Association for Computational Linguistics (Volume 1: Long Papers)*, volume 1, pages 435–445.

Shashi Narayan, Claire Gardent, Shay B Cohen, and Anastasia Shimorina. 2017. Split and rephrase. *arXiv preprint arXiv:1707.06971*.

Kishore Papineni, Salim Roukos, Todd Ward, and Wei-Jing Zhu. 2002. Bleu: a method for automatic evaluation of machine translation. In *Proceedings of the 40th annual meeting on association for computational linguistics*, pages 311–318. Association for Computational Linguistics.

Fabian Pedregosa, Gal Varoquaux, Alexandre Gramfort, Vincent Michel, Bertrand Thirion, Olivier Grisel, Mathieu Blondel, Peter Prettenhofer, Ron Weiss, Vincent Dubourg, Jake Vanderplas, Alexandre Passos, David Cournapeau, Matthieu Brucher, Matthieu Perrot, and douard Duchesnay. 2011. Scikit-learn: Machine Learning in Python. *Journal of Machine Learning Research*, 12:2825–2830.

Luz Rello, Ricardo Baeza-Yates, Stefan Bott, and Horacio Saggion. 2013. Simplify or help?: text simplification strategies for people with dyslexia. In *Proceedings of the 10th International Cross-Disciplinary Conference on Web Accessibility*, page 15. ACM.

Miguel Rios and Serge Sharoff. 2015. Large scale translation quality estimation. In *The Proceedings of the 1st Deep Machine Translation Workshop*.

Horacio Saggion, Elena Gómez Martínez, Esteban Etayo, Alberto Anula, and Lorena Bourg. 2011. Text simplification in simplext. making text more accessible. *Procesamiento del lenguaje natural*, 47:341–342.

Max Schwarzer and David Kauchak. 2018. Human evaluation for text simplification: The simplicity-adequacy tradeoff.

Matthew G Snover, Nitin Madnani, Bonnie Dorr, and Richard Schwartz. 2009. Ter-plus: paraphrase, semantic, and alignment enhancements to translation edit rate. *Machine Translation*, 23(2-3):117–127.

Lucia Specia. 2010. Translating from complex to simplified sentences. In *International Conference on Computational Processing of the Portuguese Language*, pages 30–39. Springer.

Lucia Specia, Kashif Shah, Jose GC Souza, and Trevor Cohn. 2013. Quest-a translation quality estimation framework. In *Proceedings of the 51st Annual Meeting of the Association for Computational Linguistics: System Demonstrations*, pages 79–84.

Sanja Štajner, Hannah Béchara, and Horacio Saggion. 2015. A deeper exploration of the standard pb-smt approach to text simplification and its evaluation. In *Proceedings of the 53rd Annual Meeting of the Association for Computational Linguistics and the 7th International Joint Conference on Natural Language Processing (Volume 2: Short Papers)*, volume 2, pages 823–828.

Sanja Štajner, Ruslan Mitkov, and Horacio Saggion. 2014. One step closer to automatic evaluation of text simplification systems. In *Proceedings of the 3rd Workshop on Predicting and Improving Text Readability for Target Reader Populations (PITR)*, pages 1–10.

Sanja Štajner, Maja Popovic, and Hanna Béchara. 2016a. Quality estimation for text simplification. In *Proceedings of the QATS Workshop*, pages 15–21.

Sanja Štajner, Maja Popovic, Horacio Saggion, Lucia Specia, and Mark Fishel. 2016b. Shared task on quality assessment for text simplification. *Training*, 218(95):192.

Elior Sulem, Omri Abend, and Ari Rappoport. 2018a. Bleu is not suitable for the evaluation of text simplification.

Elior Sulem, Omri Abend, and Ari Rappoport. 2018b. Semantic structural evaluation for text simplification. In *Proceedings of the 2018 Conference of the North American Chapter of the Association for Computational Linguistics: Human Language Technologies, Volume 1 (Long Papers)*, volume 1, pages 685–696.

Jrg Tiedemann. 2012. Parallel Data, Tools and Interfaces in OPUS. In *Proceedings of the 8th International Conference on Language Resources and Evaluation*, LREC'12, pages 2214–2218, Istanbul, Turkey.

David Vickrey and Daphne Koller. 2008. Sentence simplification for semantic role labeling. *Proceedings of ACL-08: HLT*, pages 344–352.

Willian Massami Watanabe, Arnaldo Candido Junior, Vinícius Rodriguez Uzêda, Renata Pontin de Mattos Fortes, Thiago Alexandre Salgueiro Pardo, and Sandra Maria Aluísio. 2009. Facilita: reading assistance for low-literacy readers. In *Proceedings of the 27th ACM international conference on Design of communication*, pages 29–36. ACM.

Sander Wubben, Antal Van Den Bosch, and Emiel Krahmer. 2012. Sentence simplification by monolingual machine translation. In *Proceedings of the 50th Annual Meeting of the Association for Computational Linguistics: Long Papers-Volume 1*, pages 1015–1024. Association for Computational Linguistics.

Menglin Xia, Ekaterina Kochmar, and Ted Briscoe. 2016. Text readability assessment for second language learners. In *Proceedings of the 11th Workshop on Innovative Use of NLP for Building Educational Applications*, pages 12–22.

Wei Xu, Chris Callison-Burch, and Courtney Napoles. 2015. Problems in current text simplification research: New data can help. *Transactions of the Association of Computational Linguistics*, 3(1):283–297.

Wei Xu, Courtney Napoles, Ellie Pavlick, Quanze Chen, and Chris Callison-Burch. 2016. Optimizing statistical machine translation for text simplification. *Transactions of the Association for Computational Linguistics*, 4:401–415.

Zhemin Zhu, Delphine Bernhard, and Iryna Gurevych. 2010. A monolingual tree-based translation model for sentence simplification. In *Proceedings of the 23rd international conference on computational linguistics*, pages 1353–1361. Association for Computational Linguistics.

Improving Machine Translation of English Relative Clauses with Automatic Text Simplification

Sanja Štajner
Data and Web Science Group
University of Mannheim
Germany
stajner.sanja@gmail.com

Maja Popović
ADAPT Centre
Dublin City University
Ireland
maja.popovic@adaptcentre.ie

Abstract

This article explores the use of automatic sentence simplification as a preprocessing step in neural machine translation of English relative clauses into grammatically complex languages. Our experiments on English-to-Serbian and English-to-German translation show that this approach can reduce technical post-editing effort (number of post-edit operations) to obtain correct translation. We find that larger improvements can be achieved for more complex target languages, as well as for MT systems with lower overall performance. The improvements mainly originate from correctly simplified sentences with relatively complex structure, while simpler structures are already translated sufficiently well using the original source sentences.

1 Introduction

Text simplification (TS) was initially proposed in the late nineties as a pre-processing step that would improve machine translation (MT), information extraction (IE), and parsing (Chandrasekar et al., 1996). At that time, text simplification was done manually and focused mainly on syntactic transformations. In the last 20 years, many automatic text simplification (ATS) systems were proposed for various languages. Most of them were done with the goal of making texts more understandable to humans. The most mature systems are those proposed for English language. The initial goal of using automatic syntactic simplification for improving MT systems has been forgotten, with the only exception being the recent work of Štajner and Popović (2016), where two lexico-syntactic ATS systems were used for transforming English sentences before translating them into Serbian. The erroneous automatic simplifications were manually corrected before passing them to the MT system. Both ATS systems performed several types of simplifications, but the effects of any particular simplification type were not investigated.

Apart from being the most studied and the most correctly performed type of automatic syntactic simplification, relative clauses are known to pose difficulties for English-to-Serbian (en-sr) and English-to-German (en-de) machine translation, due to target languages being morphologically rich and with different syntactic structures than English. Two examples of English relative clauses problematic for machine translation are shown in Table 1. In the first sentence, the relative pronoun "which" is problematic. The translation is lexically correct in both target languages. However, due to incorrect gender and/or case, it does not relate to the "plot summary" as in the original sentence, but to "Lorax Film" in the German translation and to "Internet Movie Database Website" in the Serbian translation. The second sentence does not have problems directly with the relative pronoun. However, due to its complex structure, the first part of the sentence is problematic for translation into both target languages. In German, there are several mistranslations (the preposition "zu" two times and the verb "bewegen"), and in Serbian, a substantial part of the sentence is missing (the entire beginning marked bold in the English sentence).

In this work, we investigate the impact of simplification of English relative clauses on the quality of en-de and en-sr neural machine translation in three scenarios: (1) using automatic simplifications without any human intervention; (2) using minimal human intervention to filter out bad simplifications, and in those cases, use the origi-

Proceedings of the 1st Workshop on Automatic Text Adaptation (ATA), pages 39–48,
Tilburg, The Netherlands, November 8 2018.

Original	Cameron's submitted text reads in part like a plot summary of the Lorax film provided on the Internet Movie Database website, **which** begins: "In the walled city ...
MT: en→de	Camerons Text liest sich teilweise wie eine Zusammenfassung des Lorax Films auf der Website der Internet Movie Database, **der** beginnt: "In der ummauerten Stadt...
MT: en→sr	Cameron-ov podnet tekst delimično pročita kao rezime snimka Lorak filma koji se nalazi na internet stranici Internet Movie Database-a, **koja** počinje: "U gradskom zidu...
Original	**Rather than having an executive make the announcement**, Rita Masoud, a Google employee who fled Kabul with her family when she was seven years old, wrote about her personal experience.
MT: en→de	Anstatt eine Führungskraft **zu** dieser Ankündigung **zu bewegen**, schrieb Rita Masoud, eine Mitarbeiterin von Google, die mit ihrer Familie aus Kabul geflohen war, als sie sieben Jahre alt war, über ihre persönlichen Erfahrungen.
MT: en→sr	***<missing clause>*** Rita Masoud, zaposleni u Google-u koji je napustio Kabul sa svojom porodicom, kada je imala sedam godina, pisao je o svom ličnom iskustvu.

Table 1: Examples of English relative clauses problematic for en-de and en-sr machine translation.

nal source sentences instead; (3) using monolingual manual correction of automatic simplifications where necessary. We also explore in which way simplification of relative clauses can improve the quality of translations, and which types of English relative clauses pose problems to machine translation into Serbian and German.

We focus on English-to-Serbian and English-to-German machine translation, as both target languages are morphologically rich and structurally different from English.

2 Related work

2.1 Automatic Text Simplification

Automatic text simplification systems are usually divided into lexical simplification (LS) systems (e.g. (Baeza-Yates et al., 2015; Glavaš and Štajner, 2015; Paetzold and Specia, 2016)), syntactic simplification (SS) systems (e.g. (Siddharthan, 2011; Aranzabe et al., 2012; Glavaš and Štajner, 2013; Brouwers et al., 2014)), and lexico-syntactic simplification (LSS) systems (e.g. (Siddharthan and Angrosh, 2014; Saggion et al., 2015; Štajner and Glavaš, 2017)). The first group of systems (LS) is only concerned with vocabulary choices and complexity of short phrases (usually unigrams, and sometimes, shorter n-grams). The second group (SS) only simplifies the syntax by splitting long sentences containing relative clauses, coordinate and subordinate structures, transforming passive to active voice, reordering sentence constituents, etc. The third group (LSS) performs both lexical and syntactic simplification at the same time.

The current state-of-the-art lexical simplification systems are unsupervised (Glavaš and Štajner, 2015; Paetzold and Specia, 2016), and although they have a decent coverage (better than the supervised LS systems) they often lead to ungrammatical output or change of original meaning (Štajner and Glavaš, 2017). The changes in meaning are not subtle, but rather essential, and as such, those systems are suitable as a preprocessing step in machine translation only with a manual correction of their output (Štajner and Popović, 2016).

The state-of-the-art syntactic simplification systems are rule-based (Siddharthan and Angrosh, 2014; Saggion et al., 2015), and as such, provide more grammatical output, at the cost of being too conservative and often not making any changes at all. Out of all syntactic simplification operations, simplification of the relative clauses is the most studied and the most reliable one, especially for English. Therefore, in this study, we focus only on this type of transformations hoping to minimize the necessity for manually correcting simplification output.

2.2 ATS for Improving MT

Many works have so far proposed to rewrite input sentences using paraphrasing or textual entailment to improve machine translation, e.g. (Callison-Burch et al., 2006; Mirkin et al., 2009; Aziz et al., 2010; Tyagi et al., 2015). Mirkin et al. (2013a,b) go one step further, proposing an interactive tool which identifies sentences which are most likely to be translated poorly, offers possible rewritings for the human editor, and then performs translation. Although such approach requires some human post-editing effort, the effort is just monolingual (at the source side only). All these approaches, although being proposed and tested on different language pairs (English-French, English-Spanish, English-Hindu), only focus on out-of-vocabulary words, or difficult to translate shorter n-grams.

The recent work of Štajner and Popović (2016), investigated the impact of lexico-syntactic automatic text simplification systems on English-to-Serbian machine translation. They used two lexico-simplification systems: the EvLex system (Štajner and Glavaš, 2017) which performs sentence splitting, lexical substitution, and content reduction, and a "classical" lexico-syntactic system (Siddharthan and Angrosh, 2014) which performs sentence splittings and lexical substitutions. Similar to Mirkin et al. (2013a), the ATS outputs were manually inspected before feeding them into the MT system. Unlike in the work of Mirkin et al. (2013a) where human editors could just accept or reject suggested simplifications, in the work of Štajner and Popović (2016), human editors were also able to do minor revisions (correcting the tense, gender, article, etc.). Both ATS systems were found to improve fluency of the translations, and reduce the post-editing effort. The influence of particular simplification types (lexical simplification, or different types of syntactic simplification) was not investigated.

3 Methodology

We perform the following experiments:

1. We select a subset of 1000 sentences of the English test set from the WMT 2016 News translation shared task[1], with English as the original source language, focusing only on the sentences which contain relative clauses.

2. We simplify those relative clauses by the state-of-the-art freely available RegenT simplifier (Siddharthan, 2011) and retain only those that were modified by the system (a total of 106 sentences from the initial 1000).

3. We conduct human evaluation of the quality of automatic simplification, and manual correction of automatic simplification where necessary.

4. We use two English-to-Serbian and one English-to-German state-of-the-art machine translation systems to translate our set of 106 sentences, their automatic simplifications made by RegenT, and their manually corrected simplifications (in those cases where human correction was necessary).

5. We manually correct the translation output, and use two automatic scores of post-editing effort as the measures of translation quality.

6. We inspect the type of translation improvements achieved with good simplifications, and the type of relative clauses whose good quality simplifications improve or deteriorate the MT output.

score	definition
5	meaning fully preserved no grammatical errors
4	meaning fully preserved minor grammatical errors
3	meaning partially changed grammar not relevant
2	meaning substantially changed grammar not relevant
1	meaning (almost) completely changed grammar not relevant

Table 2: Guidelines for ATS evaluation

3.1 Simplification of Relative Clauses

For automatic simplification of English relative clauses, we use the state-of-the-art RegenT simplifier (Siddharthan, 2011) which is designed for text regeneration tasks such as text simplification, style modification or paraphrasing. The system applies transformation rules (specified in XML files) to a typed dependency representation obtained from the Stanford Parser (De Marneffe et al., 2006). The transformation rules were manually created, and are grouped according to the simplification operation they model: simplifying coordination, subordination, apposition and relative clauses, as well as conversion of passive to active voice. The rule files can be used in combinations or independently; for our experiments, we used only the rules for relative clauses.[2] The system keeps the entire information in the simplified sentence, it does not tend to remove any information from the original sentence, and as such it is well-suited as a preprocessing step for MT.

The quality assessment was done by three annotators, all three native English speakers. The

[1]http://www.statmt.org/wmt16/translation-task.html

[2]http://homepages.abdn.ac.uk/cgi-bin/cgiwrap/csc323/RegenT/demo.cgi, simplified in November 2017.

(1) good "5"	*meaning preserved, no grammar errors*
original	Both taught in **the Division of Social Sciences and History, which lists** 17 faculty members, and many students took courses from both.
simplified	Both taught in the Division of Social Sciences and History and many students took courses from both. **The Division lists** 17 faculty members.

(2) good "4"	*meaning preserved, two additions (comma and determiner "this")*
original	**Unlike light, which** has to be sent down an optic fibre to the desired location inside the brain, low frequency ultrasound waves can pass through tissue unhindered.
simplified	**Light**, has to be sent down an optic fiber to the desired location inside the brain. **Unlike** this **light**, low frequency ultrasound waves can pass through tissue unhindered.

(3) bad "3"	*meaning partly changed, some grammatical errors*
original	Human breast milk is composed of **a variety of proteins, fats, vitamins, and carbohydrates, which** give babies all the nutrients they need.
simplified	Human breast milk is composed of **a variety** and **fats** and **vitamins** of proteins, **carbohydrates**. **This variety** give babies all the nutrients they need.

(4) bad "2"	*meaning changed to a large extent due to lack of negation, no grammar errors*
original	There's **no consensus** about what the Fed will do, **which** in itself is causing financial market jitters .
simplified	There's **no consensus** about what the Fed will do. **This** consensus in itself is causing financial market jitters.

(5) bad "1"	*meaning changed, low grammaticality*
original	**A student who** praised **Lamb**, Brandon Beavers, said **he** also seemed agitated and jittery, " like there was something wrong with **him**. "
simplified	**A student** praised *Lamb*, Brandon Beavers, said *he* also seemed agitated and jittery, 'like there. **This student** was something wrong with *him*.'.

(6) bad ("1")	*meaning changed (wrong co-reference), no grammar errors*
original	The bubbles, he found, amplify **the ultrasonic waves which** then pass inside the worms.
simplified	The bubbles, he found, amplify **the ultrasonic waves.** The bubbles then pass inside the worms.

(7) bad ("1")	*meaning changed (all companies instead of some), no grammar errors*
original	Broadly speaking, **companies that do** the majority of their business in the U.S. will win...
simplified	**Companies** do the majority of their business in the U.S. Broadly speaking, **these companies** will win...

Table 3: Examples of good and bad simplifications and their ATS-RC scores. Related elements in a sentence are presented in bold, and erroneous parts in red.

final score was calculated as the arithmetic mean of the three scores, rounded at the closest integer. The inter-annotator agreement, calculated as the weighted Cohen's kappa, was 0.65, 0.72, and 0.62, respectively.

Seven example sentences with their scores presented in Table 3 illustrate the simplification scores and the mechanism of assigning them.

3.2 Manual Correction of Simplifications

The sentences which were assigned "bad" scores in the previous step, were manually corrected, using the minimal effort for corrections. Similar as in (Štajner and Popović, 2016; Štajner and Glavaš, 2017), the editor (native English speaker) was instructed not to introduce any additional simplifications, but rather minimally correct the output so that the original meaning and grammaticality of the sentences are preserved. The second editor (native English speaker) controlled the quality of the corrections.

3.3 Machine Translation

All original, automatically simplified, and corrected English sentences were translated into Serbian and German by the Google translate system[3] in February 2018. For the analysis of intrinsic limits of using simplification of English relative clauses as a pre-processing step for NMT, avail-

[3]https://translate.google.com/

ATS-RC score	sentences #	%	group	sentences #	%
1	37	34.9			
2	5	4.7	bad	56	52.8
3	14	13.2			
4	17	16.0	good	50	47.2
5	33	31.2			

Table 4: Distribution of simplification quality scores (with meaning preservation as the primary criterion, and grammaticality as the secondary).

ability of two distinct target languages is a big advantage, since possible influences of language-related characteristics are reduced. To avoid possible dependencies on the MT system, translations produced by another publicly available NMT system for English-to-Serbian, Asistent[4], were included in the in-depth analyses (Section 5). In this way, two target languages of the same MT system, as well as two different systems for the same target language were taken into account.

3.4 Evaluation

Although German reference translations were available (Serbian were not, as Serbian is not among the languages investigated at the WMT shared task), using reference translations is not convenient for this type of evaluation since it would penalize too harsh the translations of simplified sentences (especially in the case of syntactic simplification involving sentence splitting and reordering of clauses). The translation outputs were post-edited minimally and the edited translations were used as reference translations to calculate two MT evaluation scores: the character n-gram F-score, chrF (Popović, 2015), and edit distance. The chrF score operates on sub-word level by matching character sequences, and it correlates very well with human direct assessment scores which are, as mentioned in Section 3.1, based mainly on adequacy and partly on fluency (Bojar et al., 2017). Edit distance represents the amount of words which have to be changed in order to transform the translation output into the reference.

4 Results and Discussion

The number and percentage of automatically simplified English clauses with each of the five possible quality scores is presented in Table 4. The sentences were further grouped into two broader

[4]http://server1.nlp.insight-centre.org/asistent/

	chrF / edit rate original	chrF / edit rate simplified
en-sr	**85.2 / 15.9**	83.0 / 20.8
en-de	**93.3 / 7.01**	89.7 / 12.8

Table 5: chrF / edit rate for Serbian and German translations of all original English sentences and all their automatic simplifications (higher chrF scores and lower edit rates indicate better translations).

		chrF / edit rate original	chrF / edit rate simplified
en-sr	good	84.6 / 16.0	**86.7 / 14.6**
	bad	**85.8 / 15.8**	79.5 / 26.4
en-de	good	92.6 / 8.05	**92.9 / 7.81**
	bad	**94.0 / 6.04**	86.5 / 17.4

Table 6: chrF score / edit rate for translations of good, and bad simplifications of English sentences into Serbian and into German. For each group, better scores are presented in bold.

categories, "good" and "bad": scores 4 and 5 are considered as good, the rest as bad.

4.1 Impact of Automatic Simplifications

The two MT scores, chrF and edit rate, are presented in Table 5 for the translations of all original and all automatically simplified English sentences (without any quality control or manual corrections). Passing the automatically simplified sentences to MT system, without any quality analysis or manual correction, seems to deteriorate the quality of translations. This can be intuitively expected, since a number of simplifications contains major errors, as shown in Table 4.

The scores for the German translations are better than for Serbian translations, probably due to Serbian being morpho-syntactically more complex language with fewer resources than German.

4.2 Impact of Simplification Quality

To explore the influence of simplification quality on translation quality, MT scores were calculated separately for the translations of good simplifications, and the translations of bad simplifications (Table 6). As expected, the simplification quality of a source sentence has a strong influence on the machine translation output: good simplifications improve the MT scores, whereas bad simplifications clearly deteriorate them. These results indicate that automatic simplification can improve machine translation of English relative clauses into Serbian and German, if we introduce a quick quality check of automatic simplifications, either human (could also be just binary assess-

	chrF / edit rate		
	original	automatic	corrected
en-sr	85.2 / 15.9	83.0 / 20.8	**86.4 / 9.4**
en-de	**93.3** / 7.01	89.7 / 12.8	**93.3 / 4.5**

Table 7: chrF / edit rate for translations of all original English sentences, all automatic simplifications, and automatic simplifications with manual corrections into Serbian and into German (the higher chrF scores and the lower edit rates, better the translations).

ment as "good"/"bad") or automatic (automatically checking meaning preservation and grammaticality). Even the first option, the human assessment, improves MT as it requires faster and less demanding (monolingual only) human intervention than post-editing of the MT output.

4.3 Impact of Automatic Simplifications with Manual Corrections

When the bad simplifications are corrected,[5] the MT scores for Serbian translation output improve, whereas for German they reach the original values by chrF scores, and improve on edit rate scores (Table 7). Taking into account the overall better performance of the English-to-German MT system, the results indicate that ATS is more helpful for translating into more complex and less supported languages (like Serbian).

We further calculated the percentages of improved, deteriorated and unchanged machine translated sentences in terms of both MT evaluation scores (Table 8). The results confirm that the influence of simplification quality is substantial. In English-to-Serbian translation, 84%–88% of bad simplifications deteriorate the translations. At the same time, only 30-50% of correctly simplified source sentences (either directly by the ATS system or by manual correction afterwards), improve the translations. The percentage of improved translations is higher for translations into Serbian, and the percentage of deteriorated translations is slightly higher for translations into German. These results are also consistent with our previous findings (Štajner and Popović, 2016), that only a subset of (correctly) simplified sentences improves the MT output. These results indicate that there are certain limits of current ATS systems when used for MT as the target application. These limitations seem not to be related to the quality of

[5]Erroneous simplifications in our set required technical post-editing effort (edit rate) of 14.2%, of which 9.2% were lexical edits and 5.0% reordering edits.

(a) en→sr

chrF	better	worse	same
good	**26 / 52.0%**	**19 / 38.0%**	5 / 10.0%
bad	9 / 16.1%	47 /83.9 %	0 / 0%
corrected	**29 / 51.8%**	**21 / 37.5%**	6 / 10.7%

edit rate	better	worse	same
good	**24 / 48.0%**	**21 / 42.0%**	5 / 10.0%
bad	7 / 12.5%	49 / 87.5%	0 / 0%
corrected	**28 / 50.0%**	**19 / 33.9%**	9 / 16.1%

(c) en→de

chrF	better	worse	same
good	**19 / 38.0%**	**23 / 46.0%**	8 / 16.0%
bad	7 /12.5 %	46 / 46.0 %	3 / 5.4 %
corrected	**20 / 35.7%**	**19 / 33.9%**	17 / 30.4%

edit rate	better	worse	same
good	**16 / 32.0%**	**24 / 48.0%**	10 / 20.0%
bad	4 / 7.1%	48 / 85.7%	4 / 7.1%
corrected	**19 / 33.9%**	**20 / 35.7%**	17 / 30.4%

Table 8: Number / percentage of improved, deteriorated and unchanged machine translated sentences in terms of the chrF score (above) and edit rate (below). Results for translations of correct (good and corrected) simplifications are presented in bold.

produced simplifications, because in all scenarios only a subset of correctly simplified sentences improves the MT output.

5 In-Depth Analysis

In order to explore the limits of simplification of English relative clauses for improving MT systems, we manually analyzed translations of all good and corrected simplifications. In this set of experiments, we used an additional English-to-Serbian MT system, as explained in Section 3.

Table 9 shows the amount of improved, deteriorated and unchanged translations when translating only the correctly simplified source sentences (either being correctly automatically simplified, or being manually corrected). For both English-to-Serbian MT systems, about a half of the simplified sentences improves the MT scores, whereas for English-to-German, improvement is achieved for only about one third of sentences. These results indicate that it is difficult to improve a very strong MT system by simplifying relative clauses. Surprisingly, even for the system with the lowest overall performance (Asistent), half of the correctly simplified sentences exhibit worse or unchanged MT scores.

In order to get more details about the two groups

chrF	better	worse	same
sr (Google)	**55 / 51.9%**	40 / 37.7%	11 / 10.4%
sr (Asistent)	**51 / 48.1%**	54 / 50.9%	1 / 1.0%
de (Google)	39 / 36.8%	**42 / 39.6%**	25 / 23.6%

edit rate	better	worse	same
sr (Google)	**52 / 49.0%**	40 / 37.7%	14 / 13.2%
sr (Asistent)	**53 / 50.0%**	51 / 48.1%	2 / 1.9%
de (Google)	35 / 33.0%	**44 / 41.5%**	27 / 25.5%

Table 9: Number / percentage of improved, deteriorated and unchanged translations in terms of the chrF score (above) and edit rate (below) for translation of good and corrected simplifications.

three types of edit rates (%)		better		worse	
		orig.	simp.	orig.	simp.
sr (Google)	inflection	5.8	**3.5**	**2.5**	3.7
	order	2.0	**1.2**	**0.9**	1.7
	lexical	12.3	**8.3**	**9.8**	13.2
sr (Asistent)	inflection	8.0	**7.8**	**7.7**	7.9
	order	8.0	**6.6**	**6.7**	7.2
	lexical	32.9	**30.9**	**30.2**	32.4
de (Google)	inflection	1.2	**0.5**	**0.4**	1.2
	order	1.2	**0.4**	**0.7**	1.5
	lexical	9.6	**3.8**	**4.1**	9.2

Table 10: Three classes of edit rates (inflectional, ordering and lexical) for improved and deteriorated translations when translating good and corrected simplifications. For each group, better scores are presented in bold.

	better	worse	same
sr (Google) ∩ sr (Asistent)	27	20	1
sr (Google) ∩ de (Google)	21	23	6
sr (Asistent) ∩ de (Google)	18	19	1

Table 11: Number of source sentences whose simplification improves/deteriorates/does not change the MT scores for different MT systems. The numbers in parentheses denote the number of corresponding sentences in each of the two involved translation outputs.

of translation outputs, improved and worsened, we performed error classification using Hjerson (Popović, 2011). Hjerson classifies the errors into five categories: inflection, order, omission, addition and mistranslation, but with a high level of confusions between omissions, additions and mistranslations. Therefore we applied the same tactic as Toral and Sánchez-Cartagena (2017), merging additions, omissions and mistranslations into one "lexical" category. The three classes of edit rates are presented in Table 10.

All three error categories are improved in "better" translations and deteriorated in "worse" translations. For the system with high overall MT score (Google), the largest changes are in the number of lexical errors. For the system with lower overall MT score (Asistent), the changes in reordering (syntactic) errors are larger and the changes in lexical errors smaller than for the better performing system (Google). Grammatical errors in the Asistent translations are much more frequent than in the Google translations, and these errors can be reduced by syntactic simplification of relative clauses. The amount of errors in translations of original versions of "better" sentences is higher than for "worse" sentences. This suggests that the MT systems can already handle the "worse" sentences sufficiently well, so that the simplification only introduces confusion which results in increased number of lexical errors.

These error rates shed some light on differences between improved and worsened translation outputs, but they did not provide any information about the corresponding source sentences.

We investigated what the source sentences (correct simplifications), both those that improve and those that deteriorate MT output, have in common regardless of the MT system and the target language. The number of such overlapping source sentences between each pair of translation outputs is presented in Table 11. The smallest overlap can be noted between German Google translations and Serbian Asistent translations, which can be expected since in this case both the target language and the MT system differ.

Several examples of improved and deteriorated sentences are presented in Table 12. Relatively simple structures where the relative pronoun, or determiner, almost immediately follows its corresponding noun are already well handled by MT systems. Simplifying such structures only introduces disturbances, which are mostly manifested in the form of increased number of lexical errors (see Table 10). More complex structures with distant relative pronouns and/or more than one possible co-reference are more difficult to translate correctly and these are the structures where simplification of relative clauses generally helps, independently of the language pair and the MT system.

Table 13 represents the most frequent POS 4-grams for the source sentences which lead to "better" and "worse" translations. Both tables clearly indicate that the structure of the sentences in the two groups differs.

(a) English sentences for which TS improves the MT scores

orig.	**A student** who praised Lamb, **Brandon Beavers**, said he also seemed agitated and jittery, "like there was something wrong with him."
simp.	**A student Brandon Beavers** who praised Lamb, said he also seemed agitated and jittery," like there was something wrong with him."
orig.	Cameron's submitted text reads in part like **a plot summary** of the Lorax film provided on the Internet Movie Database website, **which** begins: "In the walled city of Thneed-Ville, where everything is artificial and even the air is a commodity, a boy named Ted hopes to win the heart of his dream girl, Audrey."
simp.	Cameron's submitted text reads in part like **a plot summary** of the Lorax film provided on the Internet Movie Database website. **The summary** begins: 'In the walled city of Thneed-Ville, where everything is artificial and even the air is a commodity, a boy named Ted hopes to win the heart of his dream girl, Audrey.'
orig.	Rather than having an executive make the announcement, **Rita Masoud, a Google employee who** fled Kabul with her family when she was seven years old, wrote about her personal experience.
simp.	**A Google employee** fled Kabul with her family when she was seven years old. Rather than having an executive make the announcement, **Rita Masoud, this employee**, wrote about her personal experience.

(b) English sentences for which TS deteriorates the MT scores

orig.	Experts believe shoppers could be holding off making purchases ahead of **the event, which** takes place on the last Friday in November.
simp.	Experts believe shoppers could be holding off making purchases ahead of **the event**. **The event** takes place on the last Friday in November.
orig.	The tiny nematodes change direction the moment they are blasted with **sonic pulses that** are too high-pitched for humans to hear.
simp.	The tiny nematodes change direction the moment they are blasted with **sonic pulses. These** pulses are too high-pitched for humans to hear.
orig.	Human breast milk is composed of **a variety** of proteins, fats, vitamins, and carbohydrates, **which** give babies all the nutrients they need.
simp.	Human breast milk is composed of **a variety** of proteins, fats, vitamins, and carbohydrates. **This variety** gives babies all the nutrients they need.

Table 12: Examples of English source sentences whose simplification (a) improves MT scores for distinct MT systems and (b) deteriorates MT scores for distinct MT systems.

effect on MT scores:	
better	worse
, N N ,	PREP DET N PREP
N PREP N ,	N , WH-DET V-PRES
PREP DET ADJ N	N PREP DET N
DET ADJ N PREP	DET N PREP N

Table 13: Most frequent POS 4-grams in the two groups of overlapping original English source sentences.

6 Summary and outlook

In this work, we showed (on a small data set) that the automatic simplification of English relative clauses can improve English-to-Serbian and English-to-German machine translation (MT) if used as a pre-processing step before translating the sentences with a neural machine translation (NMT) system, only if used with the quality control of the simplifications, or some minimal manual correction of the simplifications. We found that such simplifications improve the output of Google's English-to-Serbian and English-to-German MT mostly by decreasing the number of lexical errors, while the output of the lower performing English-to-Serbian NMT system (Asistent) mostly benefit from a decreased number of reordering errors. We also found that both target languages and both MT systems share the patterns of relative clauses whose simplification improves the translations. The described limitations of using simplification of English relative clauses for improving MT output are not surprising: the state-of-the-art ATS systems were tailored for improving comprehension of texts by different target users. Those transformations do not necessarily coincide with improving machine translation. An important direction for future work is to develop ATS systems which are tailored for structures problematic for MT.

Acknowledgements: This research was supported by the ADAPT Centre for Digital Content Technology at Dublin City University, funded under the Science Foundation Ireland Research Centres Programme (Grant 13/RC/2106) and co-funded under the European Regional Development Fund.

References

María Jesús Aranzabe, Arantza Díaz De Ilarraza, and Itziar González. 2012. First Approach to Automatic Text Simplification in Basque. In *Proceedings of the first Natural Language Processing for Improving Textual Accessibility Workshop (NLP4ITA 2012)*, Istanbul, Turkey.

Wilker Aziz, Marc Dymetman, Shachar Mirkin, Lucia Specia, Nicola Cancedda, and Ido Dagan. 2010. Learning an expert from human annotations in statistical machine translation: the case of out-of-vocabulary words. In *Proceedings of EAMT*.

Ricardo Baeza-Yates, Luz Rello, and Julia Dembowski. 2015. Cassa: A context-aware synonym simplification algorithm. In *Proceedings of the 2015 Conference of the North American Chapter of the Association for Computational Linguistic and Human Language Technologies (NAACL-HLT 2015)*, pages 1380–1385, Denver, Colorado.

Ondřej Bojar, Rajen Chatterjee, Christian Federmann, Yvette Graham, Barry Haddow, Matthias Huck, Antonio Jimeno Yepes, Philipp Koehn, Varvara Logacheva, Christof Monz, Matteo Negri, Aurelie Neveol, Mariana Neves, Martin Popel, Matt Post, Raphael Rubino, Carolina Scarton, Lucia Specia, Marco Turchi, Karin Verspoor, and Marcos Zampieri. 2016. Findings of the 2016 Conference on Machine Translation. In *Proceedings of the First Conference on Machine Translation (WMT 2016)*, pages 131–198, Berlin, Germany.

Ondřej Bojar, Yvette Graham, and Amir Kamran. 2017. Results of the WMT17 Metrics Shared Task. In *Proceedings of the Second Conference on Machine Translation (WMT 2017)*, pages 489–513, Copenhagen, Denmark.

Laetitia Brouwers, Delphine Bernhard, Anne-Laure Ligozat, and Thomas François. 2014. Syntactic sentence simplification for french. In *Proceedings of the 3rd Workshop on Predicting and Improving Text Readability for Target Reader Populations (PITR)*, pages 47–56, Gothenburg, Sweden.

Chris Callison-Burch, Philipp Koehn, and Miles Osborne. 2006. Improved statistical machine translation using paraphrases. In *Proceedings of the 2016 Human Language Technology Conference of the North American Chapter of the ACL (HLT-NAACL)*, pages 17–24.

Raman Chandrasekar, Christine Doran, and B. Srinivas. 1996. Motivations and Methods for Text Simplification. In *Proceedings of COLING 1996*, pages 1041–1044, Copenhagen, Denmark.

Marie-Catherine De Marneffe, Bill McCartney, and Christopher Manning. 2006. Generating Typed Dependency Parses from Phrase Structure Parses. In *Proceedings of the Fifth International Conference on Language Resources and Evaluation (LREC 2006)*, pages 449–454, Genoa, Italy.

Goran Glavaš and Sanja Štajner. 2013. Event-Centered Simplication of News Stories. In *Proceedings of the Student Workshop at RANLP 2013*, pages 71–78, Hissar, Bulgaria.

Goran Glavaš and Sanja Štajner. 2015. Simplifying Lexical Simplification: Do We Need Simplified Corpora? In *Proceedings of the ACL&IJCNLP 2015 (Volume 2: Short Papers)*, pages 63–68, Beijing, China.

Shachar Mirkin, Lucia Specia, Nicola Cancedda, Ido Dagan, Marc Dymetman, and Idan Szpektor. 2009. Source-language entailment modeling for translating unknown terms. In *Proceedings of the Joint Conference of the 47th Annual Meeting of the ACL and the 4th International Joint Conference on Natural Language Processing of the AFNLP: Volume 2 - Volume 2*, ACL '09, pages 791–799, Stroudsburg, PA, USA. Association for Computational Linguistics.

Shachar Mirkin, Sriram Venkatapathy, and Marc Dymetman. 2013a. Confidence-driven Rewriting for Improved Translation. In *Proceedings of the XIV MT Summit, Nice, France*, pages 257–264.

Shachar Mirkin, Sriram Venkatapathy, Marc Dymetman, and Ioan Calapodescu. 2013b. SORT: An Interactive Source-Rewriting Tool for Improved Translation. In *Proceedings of ACL, Sofia, Bulgaria*, pages 85–90.

Gustavo Henrique Paetzold and Lucia Specia. 2016. Unsupervised lexical simplification for non-native speakers. In *Proceedings of the 30th Conference on Artificial Intelligence (AAAI 2016)*, Phoenix, Arizona.

Maja Popović. 2011. Hjerson: An Open Source Tool for Automatic Error Classificatio n of Machine Translation Output. *The Prague Bulletin of Mathematical Linguistics*, (96):59–68.

Maja Popović. 2015. chrF: Character n-gram F-score for Automatic MT Evaluation. In *Proceedings of the 10th Workshop on Statistical Machine Translation (WMT 2015)*, pages 392–395, Lisbon, Portugal.

Horacio Saggion, Sanja Štajner, Stefan Bott, Simon Mille, Luz Rello, and Biljana Drndarevic. 2015. Making It Simplext: Implementation and Evaluation of a Text Simplification System for Spanish. *ACM Transactions on Accessible Computing*, 6(4):14:1–14:36.

Advaith Siddharthan. 2011. Text simplification using typed dependencies: a comparison of the robustness of different generation strategies. In *Proceedings of the 13th European Workshop on Natural Language Generation (ENLG 2011)*, page 2–11, Nancy, France.

Advaith Siddharthan and M. A. Angrosh. 2014. Hybrid text simplification using synchronous dependency grammars with hand-written and automatically harvested rules. In *Proceedings of the 14th Conference of the European Chapter of the Association for Computational Linguistics (EACL 2014)*, pages 722–731, Gothenburg, Sweden.

Antonio Toral and Víctor Manuel Sánchez-Cartagena. 2017. A Multifaceted Evaluation of Neural versus Statistical Machine Translation for 9 Language Directions. In *Proceedings of the 15th Conference of the European Chapter of the Association for Computational Linguistics (EACL 2017)*, Valencia, Spain.

Shruti Tyagi, Deepti Chopra, and Iti Mathur. 2015. Classifier based text simplification for improved machine translation. In *Proceedings of International Conference on Advances in Computer Engineering and Applications (ICACEA), Ghaziabad, India*, pages 46–50.

Sanja Štajner and Goran Glavaš. 2017. Leveraging event-based semantics for automated text simplification. *Expert Systems with Applications*, 82:383–395.

Sanja Štajner and Maja Popović. 2016. Can text simplification help machine translation? In *Proceedings of the 19th Annual Conference of the European Association for Machine Translation (EAMT 2016)*, pages 230–242, Riga, Latvia.

Author Index